"In *Reconstructed*, Amanda gives her audience a front row seat to her struggle with body image, success, and identity. In each chapter she beautifully explains how the Holy Spirit reconstructed her identity by applying the truths of Jesus' birth, death, and resurrection. She brags on her Savior and shows how He offers ultimate fulfillment to all people. Amanda is a student of psychology and offers valuable insight into how our brain processes events and information. In this book she incorporates her knowledge and demonstrates how it helped her process her trauma and identity issues. If you are weary from trying to find your identity in personal appearance or self-worth through success, this book is for you."

—Tracy Richardson

Church planter's wife, author of *The Sermon on the Mount: A 31 Day Guide through Jesus' Teaching*

I0211560

"Amanda Rutledge's book *Reconstructed* offers her readers a unique glimpse into the life and thought patterns of someone who has suffered much trauma yet emerged from that trauma reconstructed into a beautiful and glorious image of Jesus Christ. The same hope Amanda found in her journey of healing she offers to her readers, while showing accurately and specifically how the gods and the remedies of this world do not satisfy. If you, like Amanda, have suffered from drinking at the fountain of the world, numbing your heart, and dulling its aches, only to wake up and discover how very thirsty you actually are, let Amanda's book lead you to the only truth that can satisfy and quench the thirst of every hurt, every trauma, and every need. Reading *Reconstructed* is choosing to walk down a road that leads to recovery and resurrection."

—Susannah Baker
author of *Waiting on the Lord* and *Known*

"Amanda is relatable, vulnerable, and encouraging. Through the story of her tragic car accident, she shares timeless truths that beckon us to stand firm and free in who we are in Christ. Amanda's journey of healing had far less to do with her body and far more to do with her soul. She so beautifully calls us to see ourselves as God does: broken, but made perfect by Christ's finished work."

—Meg Marie Wallace
wife, mom, author, fitness model, blogger
megmariewallace.com

Reconstructed

Finding Christian Identity
in a Postmodern World

Amanda
Rutledge

LUCIDBOOKS

Reconstructed

Finding Christian Identity in a Postmodern World

Copyright © 2017 by Amanda Rutledge

Back cover photo: Elisabeth Carol Photography

Published by Lucid Books in Houston, TX
www.LucidBooksPublishing.com

ISBN 10: 1632961539
ISBN 13: 9781632961532
eISBN 10: 1632961547
eISBN 13: 9781632961549

Unless otherwise noted, Scripture quotations are from the ESV® Bible (The Holy Bible, English Standard Version©), copyright © 2001 by Crossway, a publishing ministry of Good News Publishers. Used by permission. All rights reserved.

Scripture quotations marked (NIV) are taken from the Holy Bible, New International Version®, NIV®. Copyright © 1973, 1978, 1984, 2011 by Biblica, Inc.™ Used by permission of Zondervan. All rights reserved worldwide. www.zondervan.com The "NIV" and "New International Version" are trademarks registered in the United States Patent and Trademark Office by Biblica, Inc.™

Special Sales: Most Lucid Books titles are available in special quantity discounts. Custom imprinting or excerpting can also be done to fit special needs. Contact Lucid Books at Info@ LucidBooksPublishing.com.

Table of Contents

Introduction

The last few hours had been blissful and perfect: seeing dolphins, staring at sunsets in the Destin Harbor, and watching fireworks blast off from a boat only a hundred or so yards away. But now it was time to leave, and leaving was when everything went wrong. Our family friend had volunteered to drive, so he slid behind the wheel of our Jeep while my stepdad climbed into the passenger seat. In the back sat my mom on the right, my 14-year-old sister in the middle, and me on the left.

Soon enough, our Jeep was picking up speed to 50 miles per hour against the shiny black tar of the highway. I leaned over to my mom and sister, showing them pictures from the evening. We laughed at the goofy ones and smiled at the ones where we all looked thinnest.

Then it happened.

Our driver cursed, and I looked up to see headlights turning in our direction. The Jeep jerked to the left, and my sister shrieked as a flash of red rammed against us. My body slammed against the interior side of the Jeep once, then twice.

The Jeep halted on the shoulder, facing lights from oncoming traffic.

The first thing I heard after we stopped was my little sister crying and repeating, "I love you." But it was her blurt of "I see smoke—get out of the car" that jolted my adrenaline. Immediately, I unbuckled the seatbelt and stumbled out of the battered vehicle and onto the grassy side of the road, falling after only a few steps.

That's when the pain in my left side came. It stabbed my chest, stealing my breath and increasing in intensity each second. As I processed the fact that the pain could be coming from any major organ, I froze, not wanting to move and somehow jeopardize my health any further.

While I tried keeping my breathing steady, I saw my sister lumber a few yards away from me, falling in the grass and sobbing. My mom came next, except she fell next to me, hysterical.

I whispered that I couldn't breathe, and her cries grew louder, turning into prayers. Closing my eyes, I could also feel that something was wrong with my left eye.

I held my mom's hands and told her everything was going to be okay, even though I could hardly breathe now. Only shallow breaths came through my throbbing lungs. My left side was in the most excruciating pain I had ever felt. Maybe my heart or lungs were punctured. Maybe this day was my last on earth.

Then I heard a strange voice coming from someone I didn't know. It was a man who had witnessed the accident and pulled over to see if we were okay. Instead of walking away, he asked if he could pray for me.

He prayed healing over me while we waited for an ambulance to arrive. I hardly remember the tone of his voice, and I never saw his face, but I will never forget the Lord's mighty way of working through that stranger's prayer.

In the next minute, the pain intensified significantly, and I asked where the ambulances were. On cue, the sirens sounded, and in minutes, the EMTs arrived.

They coaxed me to roll from my right side on the edge of the road to my back on the stretcher. I hardly felt my skin rip away from the blades of grass that had begun to stick to my skin. Instead, all I felt was the strain in my chest, constricting my breathing and narrowing my thoughts. But the EMTs were there, redirecting my focus from the pain to the next step that would get me closer to safety. Even if I could not make eye contact with them or speak to them, I could feel their urgency in the even tones of their voices.

The blood slid from somewhere around my left eye down my cheek, and I wondered where the cut was. I saw my mom and the fear in her eyes. I may not have seen the EMTs, but their deliberate pauses and controlled voices cut through my mom's cries and fueled my uncertainty.

I had never been on a stretcher before. I had seen them on television and at the scenes of some accidents, but I had never pictured myself actually lying on the blue and yellow support that carried me from the side of the road to the safety of an ambulance. As the EMTs counted from three, two, one, then lifted me from lying on the ground to lying in the air, I felt my stomach turn with a surreal twist. I focused on the spinning red and blue lights and the blaring sirens that came from the ambulance that I imagined would save my life. Holding my breath, I knew the next few seconds would either bring me some relief or cause me to continue holding onto the breath inside my throbbing lungs.

"Vitals are normal," one of them said, and I breathed a painful sigh of relief as we traveled the few minutes to the nearest hospital.

Despite the intense nature of the incident, processes at the hospital dragged out. The wait was excruciating for me, but worse for my worried mother who'd taken a hard beating herself. My sister had a broken collarbone, and the nurses were wrapping up her arm.

But problems for me couldn't be wrapped in a bandage. With two broken ribs and a lacerated liver, I needed transport to a more advanced hospital. I soon found myself on another stretcher in another ambulance where I endured an hour-long ride, stressing under the occasional tightness in my chest and wondering how long my liver would hold out.

Miraculously, I did not need surgery. Even though I had a lacerated liver, two broken ribs, a broken lateral side wall (which holds the eye in place), only a few eyelashes on my left eyelid, bruised lungs, and a permanently damaged kidney, I could leave the Florida hospital without having any incisions. The recovery would be long, but I would recover. However, the recovery was more painful than I had anticipated and in ways I had never imagined.

Before the wreck ruined my body on physical and mental levels, I had placed my joy in my beauty. The summer of freedom between graduating from college and starting graduate school had freed me from time constraints and allowed me to exercise freely, sunbathe regularly, and eat healthy meals consistently. As a result, I had perfected my regimen and my figure. Moving to a new city, buzzing with bars and boys, also gave a way for me to spend most of my weekends searching for approval and getting it easily.

Except the search turned up empty weekend after weekend, leaving me longing for more once Monday came around. The fun was fleeting and ephemeral.

Many of the struggles I faced during the summer of the car wreck derived from an instinctive inclination to listen to and believe lies about myself. But these lies extended beyond summers of partying.

The Bible tells us that Satan "does not stand in truth, because there is no truth in him. When he lies, he speaks out of his own character, for he is a liar and the father of lies" (John 8:44). However, Satan also "disguises himself as an angel of light" (2 Corinthians 11:14), which makes distinguishing between truth and lies difficult.

In all stages of life, we formulate our identity on both lies and truth. Our hope, joy, and peace fluctuate because we fail to base our sense of self on a foundation of truth. Attempts to find a sense of self by trial and error result in more error than success.

To find and uphold an identity that is concrete, we have to discover what is concrete to begin with. After the accident, I began graduate school to become a counselor. I learned about two theories in particular that can help us understand identity. Although social constructionism and constructivism are not divine truth, some tenets of these theories make a lot of sense when paired with the truths of what God says in the Bible about who we are in light of who He is. Understanding both these theories and the Bible shattered my sense of security in the lies I had believed and opened my eyes to the unstable ground on which I had placed my identity.

The wreck completely altered the way I saw identity, but God revealed His faithfulness to me by teaching me truth upon truth from my experiences before, during, and after the wreck. Each truth aligns with different elements of certain postmodern theories and how I now understand the type of identity that remains intact when all other foundations begin to crumble.

Part One

Power of Perception

Chapter One
Contacts and Context

During the month after the accident, my gratitude for being alive was dulled by the tormenting thoughts plaguing my mind: How could I be skinny if I could not even exercise?

This thought began my crisis with identity. Who was I? What was I worth if I didn't turn heads when I entered a room? At the time, I didn't recognize the core issues I was dealing with because I was so consumed with my outward identity. My thoughts traveled to treadmills and diets to the point of panic.

Treadmills now exhausted me in a matter of minutes. Exercise was a hopeless endeavor, so instead I entertained dark thoughts. I had heard of women and girls struggling with eating disorders; I knew it was unsafe and not honoring to the body God had given me, but still the allure of losing the excess weight was strong, pulling me toward my apartment's bathroom.

I knew I could not be anorexic, for, frankly, I like food too much. And I like cooking. Working part-time over the summer, I had extra hours of free time to cook. I enjoyed learning new recipes, and I relished relaxing evenings by the television. No, I couldn't give up food.

Instead, I considered bulimia. I told myself I would be smart about it, only purging occasionally as to not permanently damage my body. I did not want it to become a disorder or anything dramatic like that; I just wanted to lose a few pounds while I couldn't work out. I told myself I would cease the purging and return to forging ahead with exercise after I finished healing.

I had never purged before, but I was willing to try. Hesitantly, I found myself on my knees, kneeling over the toilet and trying to induce myself to vomit.

After a few brief attempts, however, I realized that I could not actually purge anything. Perhaps my body was not wired that way, or perhaps God was intervening. Either way, after several minutes, I stopped trying and tears burst out of nowhere. I was disgusted with myself for doing such an abhorrent thing. Yet now I realized that I had been looking at my problem from the wrong angle.

For the past few weeks, I had told numerous people the story of my family's survival, and in every telling, I had given God the glory for saving us. However, I had not given God the glory in my heart. I had become bitter with my circumstances and unhappy with my body.

Hopelessness is a hard battle because it stems from a belief system that stresses extremes. Because I believed my situation to be unbearable, I perceived my body to be irreparable. I had set my mind on things that pertained to my flesh rather than to godliness:

> *For those who live according to the flesh set their minds on the things of the flesh, but those who live according to the Spirit set their minds on the things of the Spirit. For to set the mind on the flesh is death, but to set the mind on the Spirit is life and peace. For the mind that is set on the flesh is hostile to God, for it does not submit to God's law; indeed, it cannot. Those who are in the flesh cannot please God. You, however, are not in the flesh but in the Spirit, if in fact the Spirit of God dwells in you. Anyone who does not have the Spirit of Christ does not belong to him. <u>But if Christ is in you, although the body is dead because of sin, the Spirit is life because of righteousness.</u> If the Spirit of him who raised Jesus from the dead dwells in you, <u>he who raised Christ Jesus from the dead will also give life to your mortal bodies through his Spirit who dwells in you.</u>*
>
> Romans 8:5–11 (emphasis added)

Jesus has given His children the Holy Spirit (John 16:7; Acts 2:38), so we can trust that the Spirit can grant us life and peace. When we set our minds on the flesh or the things of the world (thinking/doing things that are dishonorable to God), we feel the repercussions of our thoughts. However, when we set our minds on what is eternal and pleasing to God, then we will reap the rewards of life.

When we focus on the blessings in our lives, we will begin to see how blessed we are.

When we focus on the blessings in our lives, we will begin to see how blessed we are. But what is even more life-giving is to orient our lives to the Blesser rather than solely the blessings, for blessings are bleak if they come from anything but the perfect and holy God. As James 1:17 says, "Every good gift and every perfect gift is from above."

When we believe that God has blessed us, we will begin to see His blessings and, ultimately, the greatest blessing of all: Himself. The only way we can experience life and peace is through Jesus Christ, who descended from heaven to live a perfect human life and die on our behalf to atone for our sins. That fact alone should be reason enough to celebrate rather than complain.

No longer was I looking at my body and hating its imperfections, but instead I was looking at Jesus and seeing His perfect sacrifice for my sake.

As I developed a clearer understanding of what God had done for me, I finally began to see my situation differently. No longer was I looking at my body and hating its imperfections, but instead I was looking at Jesus and seeing His perfect sacrifice for my sake. Once I began to see my own life in light of eternity, I saw that God works all things for *His* glory and *my* good (Romans 8:28). I began to perceive my reality as something greater than myself because of my Scripture-based beliefs, resulting in looking to my Blesser and seeing the Blessing that forever saved my life.

Solution-Focused

Not long into my recovery, I entered graduate school to study counseling. Going into the first week of classes, I thought I understood how the therapy session was supposed to happen. The client sits down and tells the therapist about his or her problems, and the therapist listens, giving wise advice and empowering the client to live a more contented life.

I soon realized that therapy does *not* go that way— at least not from the solution-focused (SF) perspective. Instead, the therapy session is much more strengths-based, focusing on what is going well in clients' lives and encouraging them to do more of what works and less of what does not. Of course, SF therapy includes other riveting ideas, but the basis of the approach is to focus on solutions rather than problems. Talking about the problem only maintains the problem; discussion around solutions builds toward the desired outcome (and much more efficiently).

This approach is consistent with what God's Word says about what ways of thinking are most helpful in living lives of peace and joy. He tells us to, "Set your minds on things that are above, not on things that are on earth" (Colossians 3:2).

When we focus our minds on the Solution, we will find our solutions. As we look to God, we will find Him. God says to Jeremiah, "Then you will call upon me and come and pray to me, and I will hear you. You will seek me and find me, when you seek me with all your heart" (Jeremiah 29:12-13). These verses show that simply looking for the positive rather than the negative can aid in seeking and maintaining a better reality.

Contacts

At some point during the accident, I had lost a contact lens. For someone with 20/200 vision and no back-up contacts on a Florida vacation, I found this situation less than ideal. After trying to see with only half-vision, I decided to take out the one intact lens I had, leaving me nearly blind throughout the rest of my hospital stay and the trip back to Texas.

When I finally obtained eyeglasses, I found that the corrected eyesight was not as beneficial as I had hoped. Yes, my eyes felt much more relaxed under the comfortable 20/20 vision, but once I could see myself clearly, I did everything but relax.

I noticed the four or five eyelashes still dangling on my left eyelid and the yellow-green markings under my eye that hovered around the broken lateral side wall (the bone that holds the eye in the socket). I could see my stomach bloating from the medicines as I sat around watching movies and trying to heal.

With plenty of time on my hands, I focused on seeing what I did not like. Even when I returned to work, the summer's appeal to get outside and relax by the pool surrounded by normal-looking, athletic women continued to press my insecurities deeper into my reality.

So I spent my time comparing myself to others, seeing their flawlessness and my flaws and knowing I could do nothing to alleviate the growing insecurity about my appearance.

This experience of looking for—and finding—my physical flaws aligns with how our beliefs influence our perceptions and how we see whatever we look for. Our beliefs also influence our future perceptions and behavior.[1] Whenever I looked for extra fat around my waist, I found it piling up day after day. But when God changed my heart from self-centeredness to gratitude, what I looked for changed. My beliefs about my situation changed how I perceived my situation.

Despite how rough I looked after the wreck, the physical damage paled in comparison to how ugly my identity was before the wreck. Before, I'd found myself exercising daily, seeking fulfillment in how the pounds fell off as I built my reality around my activity level and my body image. Meanwhile, I also found myself in ungodly places talking with non-Christian crowds (and not in an evangelistic mindset). Before the accident, I was perfectly fine going on dates with multiple guys in the same week because I found joy and security in their affirmation.

I may have looked fit on the outside, but spiritually, I was weak.

And this was after completing an undergraduate degree at a private university, where I helped lead a Christian sorority. Looking back at my behavior during that summer,

I wonder how I went from being "Sorority Member of the Year" because of my godly influence to frequently partying and making poor choices.

As a single woman, I relished the looks I received and the adoration men shot my way. Spending time at the pool only demanded I look the part I was playing. The pattern became regular and circular. Exercise, go out, receive affirmation from guys, make poor choices, exercise, repeat. And the worst part was that I was content disobeying God's call for me to live above reproach; I was having fun, so I justified my behavior.

How tragically beautiful, then, was the wreck that interrupted the sick cycle of sin in which I was so irreversibly steeped.

But with this interruption came a costly price to my ego. My distorted reflection caused me to perceive myself as flawed. This perception caused me to act downcast, push my body too quickly, and falter in my faith. The continual negative actions resulted in a vicious cycle of self-pity. My perceptions and behaviors influenced my beliefs about myself, but my beliefs about my inadequacies also determined my own perception.[2] This circular concept portrays a recursive pattern that happens more often than we may think. This cyclical concept shows us the systematic way we process the world around us, and this relational idea is just a glimpse of how God Himself operates.

Systems play substantial roles in how we see ourselves in light of the rest of the world. It all dwindles down to a much more interactional way of viewing life. Rather than acting alone in the aftermath of the car accident, I interacted with many other people and forces, my "system" at the time.

This systems perspective is not inconsistent with a biblical lens. Often, I viewed the accident on some linear timeline (i.e., before the accident, during the accident, after the accident). Rarely did I pause and ponder the concept of time as systematic (i.e., what happened before the accident influenced the accident and all that happened after and in between). Even if we hold to a systems way of processing time (as though it is bigger than ourselves), we cannot fathom or see beyond the perspective that we have in our limited time on earth, just like I could not see the repercussions of the accident before the accident even happened. We understand time to pass with no infractions, and, thus we see it occurring in a linear format. It merely ticks by second after second, not rewinding or fast-forwarding. What is amazing about what the Bible says about time, though, is that God is above the linear way we process time, showing how He is the only One who can see time in its infinitely systematic format. He is the only One who could see all that He plans to do with our lives.

> *For my thoughts are not your thoughts, neither are your ways*
> *my ways, declares the Lord. For as the heavens are higher*
> *than the earth, so are my ways higher than your ways and my*
> *thoughts than your thoughts.*
>
> Isaiah 55:8–9

God understands the creation of the universe, the way America became a nation, and the manner in which the end times will occur. He knows how all our interactions will influence us to believe certain things about ourselves.

And He sees that when we listen to the world's standards of who we should be, we will forever be inadequate; but when we see Jesus taking on all our imperfections, we see our inadequacies taken captive and discarded, replaced by a spotless Savior.

We can trust that His knowledge of everything is better than our knowledge of our finite things.

We have no way to understand the intricacies of how the past, present, or future influences us the way God understands the universal system. But God knows, and we can trust that His knowledge of everything is better than our knowledge of our finite things.

Furthermore, not only does He have knowledge of the entire universe, but He is the ultimate system. The Bible informs us that He is not solitary. As we see in His triune nature, He is interactional and relational.

And it is God who establishes us with you in Christ, and has anointed us, and who has also put his seal on us and given us his Spirit in our hearts as a guarantee.

2 Corinthians 1:21–22

Contacts and Context

Grasping God's relational character[3] is essential in understanding how we develop character and identity. For right before God created man in His image (Genesis 1:27), He said, "Let *us* make man in *our* image, after *our* likeness" (Genesis 1:26; italics added). God spoke about Jesus and the Holy Spirit in this conversation (the *us* and *our* in the verse), which are all entities of Himself. God is relational and social; therefore, we are as well.

He shows us that He is bigger than us—regarding both His infinite knowledge and His complex nature. However, since we have the blessing of living as creatures in His image, we know that we, too, have complex problems. We are not simple. We do not believe certain things about ourselves simply because we choose to. People, circumstances, and culture influence us to believe both positive and negative thoughts about identity. And those beliefs cause us to look for certain things in others and ourselves to affirm those beliefs. This process could repeat an infinite number of times, revealing our substantial problems with identity, because finding a solid identity is not easy when beliefs and perceptions influence us on a daily basis.

God shows us through the Word what we are to believe and how the gospel influences our view of the world and ourselves.

Reconstructed

Nevertheless, our good news as Christians is that we have something foundational that provides us with consistent and eternal beliefs. We do not have to wonder what God thinks about us or contemplate how we should see the world. God shows us through the Word what we are to believe and how the gospel influences our view of the world and ourselves. We have security in knowing that the One who knows all and who is exceedingly complex loves us enough to provide a Book that reveals all we need to know to understand who we are.

When I began to behave differently by choosing to spend time with godly people and focusing my energy on being healthy rather than attractive, I found a different kind of happiness—joy. Before, I received flattery often, which lifted my girlish spirit, but the feelings were fleeting. And although I knew the flattery would be fleeting, my emotional needs and pride continued to keep me from fulfilling what I truly desired, which was affirmation from a godly man. After I began to base my happiness in Someone eternal, however, I began to experience joy, which does not waver because God's affirmation of me never wavers. I belong to Him and Him alone, and nothing can take that away. No lack of exercise can detract Him from seeing me as beautiful because He looks at me and sees the purity of Jesus.

Or do you not know that your body is a temple of the Holy Spirit within you, whom you have from God? You are not your own, for you were bought with a price. So glorify God in your body.

1 Corinthians 6:19–20

My behavior shifted with this piece of truth in mind. Once I could exercise again, I prioritized, not allowing the workouts to be excessive or to punish myself mentally whenever I skipped. I no longer made the gym a place of worship, but instead I used the gym to take care of the body that God created. By working out to steward my body well, I maintained a reality that included a clearer picture of my place in the universe. No longer did I behave as though I was the focal point of guys' lives and the center of my own universe; instead, I began to behave as though God was the focal point of all of life. Doing so resulted in a much more joyous and Christ-centered reality.

Context Is Key

Our contexts influence how we observe the world around us and the outcome of those observations.[4] Each person has a different context and therefore sees the world differently. My context after the accident and during my recovery included the inability to exercise. This context caused me to see other women differently. No longer did I see them as sisters in Christ or as women who had stories of resilience and power. Instead, my context caused me to judge and envy them, resulting in an outcome of disdain.

In a similar way, biblical scholars know that when reading the Bible, context is key. Rather than reading verses and immediately applying them to our own lives, we must first look at the verses in context. So we must see God's Word for what it really is, looking at the author, the time, the place it was written, and to whom the author was writing. Scholars may have many other ways to address context, but the basis of context includes understanding what the verses meant to those present at the time they were written. After we have a better understanding of the verses in context, we can then see how God wants to use them in our contexts, if the contexts are similar.

Analogous to how Bible scholars look at context to get a clearer picture of who God is, we too can view our own context in a biblical light to develop a better understanding of who we are, especially in relation to who God is.

Each person has a different context, which is part of the subjective experiences of each individual's reality. We may have similarities with others, but no two people have the exact same context. Even twins and family members have different contexts, for each person experiences the world differently from others, even if only slightly.

Furthermore, we often see the world as separate from ourselves and therefore not influential. Prior to the accident, I went about my life oblivious of how my non-biblical context was influencing me to act in non-biblical ways. I saw myself as outside the context of culture, ingrained in my own environment.

However, when I finally stepped back and saw myself as part of culture and thus influenced by culture, I saw the bigger picture. Rather than limiting my scope to my perspective, I could observe the world around me and know its ability to influence me and my ability to influence it.

One key principle used to explain this phenomenon is the Heisenberg Uncertainty Principle, which states that simply observing the world around us automatically changes the world around us, and vice versa. Even though we may not think our non-participatory involvement influences others, and vice versa, simply being part of the world automatically provides us a universal context of mutual influence. We cannot escape culture, nor can culture escape us. Although we live in a society that emphasizes radical individualism, we do not live in a bubble with no contact with other humans. Regardless of the amount of our influence or participation, we still change the dynamics simply by being present. Therefore, our context includes others and not merely ourselves. This mindset influences the kinds of observations we make and the outcomes we expect. When we see ourselves from a biblical standpoint, we know we are part of a divine plan despite our earthly context.

In [Jesus] we have redemption through his blood, the forgiveness of our trespasses, according to the riches of his grace, which he lavished upon us, in all wisdom and insight making known to us the mystery of his will, according to his purpose, which he set forth in Christ as a plan for the fullness of time, to unite all things in him, things in heaven and things on earth.

Ephesians 1:7–10; emphasis added

As children of God, we see ourselves working in line with God's will. Even though the *how* of His will is mysterious to us, we know that He desires to unite His people to Himself, despite the chasm that arose between us when sin entered the world (Genesis 3). He did this and continues to do this through Jesus. His work on the cross allows us to see ourselves in the context of God's eternal plan rather than a self-centered and mortal plan that ends with our death. How sweet, then, is knowing that God is working with us to accomplish His will! We are not walking alone (Hebrews 13:5); He is with us in the Holy Spirit, guiding us along the way.

> *Likewise, the Spirit helps us in our weakness. For we do not know what to pray for as we ought, but the Spirit himself intercedes for us with groanings too deep for words. And he who searches hearts knows what is the mind of the Spirit, because the Spirit intercedes for the saints according to the will of God.*
> Romans 8:26–27; emphasis added

Therefore, God is the central part of the context in which we see the world. We see His influence everywhere, whether it is in a beautiful sunset or a tragic car accident. This influence ultimately points us to the outcome of God's creation and redemption of the world. We may not know how God is going to accomplish His saving work, but we do see Him working through His Spirit among His people as part of something greater than ourselves. Because He is sovereign, He also has the ability to see us from His external perspective, something that no human can do because no one is completely solitary or omniscient.

These ideas may seem contradictory, for how could someone outside a system, who created the system, also see the system as though separate from it? Francis S. Collins, in discussing instances of miracles, references God's involvement in mortal matters: "If, like me, you admit that there might exist something or someone outside of nature, then there is no logical reason why that force could not on rare occasions stage an invasion."[5]

Thus, God entered our system when He came to earth as Jesus (the ultimate miracle), but He also continues to work among us through the Holy Spirit. However, God also has the ability to be outside our system if He so desires. For example, before we existed, God was present (Genesis 1:1–2). Thus, He had to be outside our system to create the system. We were not working alongside Him to create the universe; He did that in and of Himself simply by speaking. He also has the omniscience to see and know His sovereign plan in its entirety. As a human part of a system, we do not have a way to see ourselves outside the system across past, present, and future. But God does.

He determines the number of the stars; he gives to all of them their names. Great is our Lord, and abundant in power; his understanding is beyond measure.

Psalm 147:4–5

Although God chooses to work in our lives as an involved Father, influencing and guiding our ways through the Holy Spirit, He is still the sovereign God, who knows the world as it is. He remains completely holy and thus completely separate from the sin that infiltrates our world: "The Lord sits enthroned over the flood; the Lord sits enthroned as king forever" (Psalm 29:10). He is the only One who can be both inside and outside our system.

Given this understanding of our awesome God, we have a much clearer understanding of our own context in light of God's sovereignty. By His grace, He works in us, and that inspires observations of praise and outcomes that lead to God's greater glory and our greatest good (Romans 8:28).

Furthermore, whenever we observe something, we automatically alter its reality because its reality now consists of someone observing it. Thus, observation alters the reality of both the observed and the observer. And to have the observed, we must have an Observer. C. S. Lewis wrote:

> The position of the question, then, is like this. We want to know whether the universe simply happens to be what it is for no reason or whether there is a power behind it that makes it what it is. Since that power, if it exists, would be not one of the observed facts but a reality which makes them, no mere observation of the facts can find it. . . . The only way in which we could expect it to show itself would be inside ourselves as an influence or a command trying to get us to behave in a certain way.[6]

From this profound idea, we can learn at least two things about who we are in relation to who God is: (1) our God is influencing us within the system that includes our Creator— our Observer, and (2) we are influenced just as much by observing Him.

First, we know we have a God who is good because He causes us to be good. We are not good apart from God, but

God causes us to make good choices when He intervenes. If we as Christians are to be marked by our love for one another (John 13:35), then the only thing that makes us love is God's influence. He reveals His love through our character and our actions. When our character reflects love for ourselves and others (including God), then we know that God is at work in us. When our character reflects love for the world, then we know that our flesh is waging war in favor of successfully tempting us away from God. If we want to uphold identities found in God and God alone, then we can rest in the fact that God not only has already begun a good work in us by causing us to want to serve Him, but He also will carry out that good work to completion (Philippians 1:6).

We may come into the world as sinners prone to wander, but the more we set our minds on things above, the more we begin to look like Christ.

Second, as we develop a greater understanding of God's holiness through reading His Scripture and experiencing His power through the Holy Spirit, we begin to look different. As we interact with the goodness of God, we change as a result. We may come into the world as sinners prone to wander, but the more we set our minds on things above, the more we begin to look like Christ.

So looking at the Heisenberg Uncertainty Principle with a Christian lens allows us to find the goodness of God abounding in His leading our own hearts to love. Because good is in the world, we know that good exists and that goodness only comes from God. As we grow in our understanding of the perfect God, we look more like Him by acting more like Him.

For those of us who are Christians striving to maintain identities that look like Christ, we can keep our lives in perspective by understanding our roles as part of God's sovereign plan. We can also use our roles to create a reality for ourselves and others that points us back to the goodness of God, which is apparent through His Word and through the good that we see in each other. Ultimately, we know that centering ourselves on Christ is possible as we acknowledge the goodness of God's influence in our otherwise bleak lives.

Reflect:

- [ ] What blessings are most important in your life today?
- [ ] What or who is the most important influence in your life right now?
- [ ] How are you shaping your current context to glorify God?

Practice:

- [ ] This first practice is an easy one: Give yourself a break. If you're anything like me, you may want to spend your days proving yourself, if not to someone else, then to yourself. Relax. You won't get it right every time, and that's okay. Rest in the fact that you are flawed just like the rest of us sinners and that a perfect Savior is taking care of you more perfectly than you ever could.

Chapter Two
Water Bottle Wisdom

Finally, my ribs stopped hurting, and I could get back to a normal workout routine. But for an outdoor lover, the treadmill was not cutting it for a new normal. With fall rolling in, I decided to join a friend of mine in training for a half-marathon. It would be a marker that I was not only back to normal but better than ever before. This race would prove that I could run 13.1 miles regardless of the wreck that had occurred only three and a half months before.

I thought I would learn something through running a half-marathon. After the injuries from the summer, I thought I could prove something by running the farthest I had ever run in my life only a few short months after the most gut-wrenching event of my life. I thought it would be a huge accomplishment—a benchmark in my own faith walk that would testify to God's grace and faithfulness to heal.

But God had a different plan.

The half-marathon was long and challenging, but I did it. I ran it in two hours and twelve minutes without walking once. I felt healthy and empowered and grateful that I was well enough to finish strong, but I did not feel suddenly or dramatically different because of this new accomplishment. Almost disappointed, I left the half-marathon without a sense of achievement, but instead with a cheap necklace, a race bib, and a water bottle.

And after running for such a long time, I was thirsty.

While driving back home, I tried to drink as much as possible to rehydrate my nutrient-depleted body. However, before I could pick up the water bottle from the passenger's seat, I found myself braking hard at a red light, sending the water bottle onto the floorboard and out of my reach.

Frustration rushed over me, my thirst escalating in a matter of seconds. Determined, I waited until I completely stopped at the next red light before I attempted to reach for the pesky bottle. Then I stretched my right arm as far as it could stretch, trying desperately to reach the water that would replenish my dehydrated body while also focusing on keeping my foot on the brake pedal. I needed the water, but it remained just out of my reach.

The light turned green, and I reluctantly looked away from the bottle and onto the road, wondering why I could not just take a drink. I had spent the last two hours depleting my body of energy, and now I could not even recover with a sip of water. Angry and pouting, I gripped the steering wheel.

Then I saw, from the corner of my eye, another water bottle sitting in my console.

I had been so unnerved by my desperation for the other water bottle that I thought would satisfy me that I had overlooked the water bottle I had brought with me prior to the race.

And then I realized, don't we do this with God?

We strive after other things that we think will satisfy us, yet we overlook what God has already provided. In desperation to find fulfillment, we look to fleshly desires and things of the world that distract us from God, and we forget to see that He has already provided our ultimate fulfillment in Him.

Even though I thought I would find fulfillment in running this monumental race, He worked in my heart through a water bottle instead.

In addition, God completely revealed that even though I thought I would find fulfillment in running this monumental race, He worked in my heart through a water bottle instead. We never know when God is going to show off His goodness and perfect plan. And even when we feel like the world has let us down, God never disappoints. Despite my search for achievement in the race and hydration in water, God showed up in a subtle yet perspective-altering way, revealing that He is sovereign and will always provide exactly what we need at the exact time we need it. He does this more often than we realize, but keeping alert to His work will allow us a higher awareness of His constant intervention.

Disordered Loves

Whenever we look at the first records of Genesis, we find that some amazing things happen when God speaks. He created the universe and all that it entails by simply using His own voice. He even created humans to have the ability to speak to each other, and a beautiful transaction occurred in Genesis 2 as Adam spoke words of praise over Eve, his bride.

However, in the next chapter, the serpent inserts his own language into the conversation, bringing sin into the mix by means of communication. Satan argues with Eve about what God had said and convinces her to disobey her Creator. Based on this transaction of language, Eve committed the first sin. She then convinced her husband to also sin by means of speaking with him, and then God revealed the consequences of sin to Adam, Eve, and Satan.

The first problem occurred through language in Genesis 3, which aligns with the fact that problems often occur in language.[1] The problem of sin would not have been apparent to Adam and Eve had they not experienced Satan communicating with them. But through language, Satan convinced them to disobey God.

Now I'm not saying that all language is sinful. As a counselor, I have seen the positive results that can occur through conversation. God's Word especially includes life-giving language, and we can often uplift each other through speaking in God-honoring language. However, whenever a problem arises, it is born from language.

We use words to convey thoughts, emotions, and everything in between. Whenever we speak and use our words, we also take a position or stance by using those words in a vocal way. We use words whenever we think and process whatever we are taking in from the external, using our words to label what our senses say is occurring.

Furthermore, whenever we process the language we hear and speak, we either find negative or positive connotations within communication transactions. Our negative or positive responses cannot occur without the language in which they lie. Therefore, problems occur through language.

But what problems do we find? Perhaps they differ for different people, but sin impacts each individual. And if sin is part of our humanity, we must know what is sinful to recognize when we are sinning and how to stop. Although I have focused most of this book on the Solution to our problems, I also want to provide a practical way of recognizing when we are placing our solutions in the wrong things.

Ryan Keeney, pastor of Grace Church Benbrook in Benbrook, Texas, explained that "sin is more than doing the wrong thing; it's loving the wrong thing."[2] So to tackle the problem of sin, we cannot just alter behavior, although behavior modification can be a good start. But for better behaviors to take root in lifestyle, we must prioritize what we love in the manner in which God intended.

Writing gives me a chance to utilize my God-given passions and find meaning in them.

For example, I love writing. Whether that writing takes the form of notes during class lectures or journaling to God or writing a book, the art and process of writing pleases my soul. When I do not write, I experience withdrawal in the form of decreased fulfillment in my life. Writing is not just a small portion of my life; it permeates how I listen to the world. Constantly, I am aware of what my pastor says, what I read, and what I hear through the media; I am always looking for something about which I can write. Writing gives me a chance to utilize my God-given passions and make meaning out of them.

However, I know that any good writing that flows from my thoughts and hands only comes from God, for every good and perfect gift is from God (James 1:17). He has blessed me with a knack for writing, so any writing that I do, I want it to glorify Him. Therefore, my love for writing must never precede my love for God.

Similarly, my love for myself must never come before my love for God.

Loving myself comes from a desire to fulfill the things that I want. It means I do what I do because I want to do it, not because it would benefit anyone else.

When I say "love for myself," I do not mean that I admire myself or have an arrogant heart (although I'll be the first to admit that I have been guilty of that). Loving myself comes from a desire to fulfill the things that I want. It means I do what I do because I want to do it, not because it would benefit anyone else. This love for self is not always bad, for God has given us confidence in whom He has created us to be. And we should show gratitude for God's use of our bodies and love that He is using us as vessels for His purposes. However, when the love of self obstructs the magnification of God's name, that is where we find a disordered love.[3] The love for self is not bad; it is just misplaced.

Not only do our sinful selves long to satisfy temptation, but our society also teaches us that everything is permissible. We learn that we can do anything we set our minds to regardless of what we have to do to get there. Although this mindset can certainly be a motivating force behind work ethic and drive, it could get tricky if the desire to achieve personal goals is elevated above the desire to please God. First Corinthians 10:23–24 says, "'All things are lawful,' but not all things are helpful. 'All things are lawful,' but not all things build up. Let no one seek his own good, but the good of his neighbor." We can work hard, but God teaches us to not work for our own glory. He teaches us to love and to work in a way that would benefit others. Thus, rather than loving ourselves and gratifying our fleshly desires that elevate our name above God's, we can love God more and show that love by placing others' needs above our own.

Sin can sprout from many sources, but the question always dwindles down to whether we love the sin more than we love God.

Sin can sprout from many sources, but the question always dwindles down to whether we love the sin more than we love God. We can place our loves in a more appropriate order by keeping God first, others second, and ourselves third.

Sin and Morality

The postmodern world may wonder why Christians label sin as bad. In a world of moral relativity, bad only exists for someone if he or she says something is bad for himself or herself. What is bad for that person, however, is not necessarily bad for someone else. Each person, in the postmodern way of thinking, can construct his or her own morality.

When Christians identify problems with the sins of others, those others may feel offended, disrespected, or annoyed, to name only a few of many probable responses. People may accuse Christians of acting as though our way of thinking is better than theirs, even though postmodernity also states that its way of thinking (that all thinking, acting, and behaving is appropriate) is best.

One does not have to do much research to see the discrepancies in the two thoughts and, thus, the rift between believers and non-believers. However, if the problem defines the system,[4] we can bring the two together to develop a better understanding of who we are. This idea basically hits on moral relativity in a sense that a problem is not a problem to those who are within the system; the problem occurs when someone outside the system identifies a problem. Those within the system may be unaffected by what the outsider labels as problematic, but the outsider still experiences a problem within the system, therefore defining the situation by its problem.

So far we have talked about systems on various levels, but in this section, I want to start by talking about the system that incorporates both Christians and non-Christians—the system that includes all of humanity—because all of us have some connection with another, regardless of the strength of that connection. Within moral relativity, we within the system do not have a problem, per se. We function within the system as though we can do no wrong because wrong is relative to each individual. However, we can agree that negative or bad things happen abundantly in life (such as war, cancer, Hitler murdering Jews, etc.). Therefore, wrong is both nonexistent and present at the same time under the postmodern umbrella; it just depends on how each individual within our system interprets that which we label as wrong.

If we hold so tightly to moral relativity that we see problems as only existent to each individual, we would have to justify Hitler's behavior as being morally right to him, even though we would say now that it was horrendous. Regardless, we are looking upon his system and labeling it as problematic even though he obviously did not see a problem with his murderous acts. His neglect of seeing a problem with his behavior does not negate the fact that it was problematic. We all—Christian and non-Christian—can agree that we would define his mass murder as wrong, regardless of his perception of his actions.

So where does the moral relativist draw the line? We have already introduced one event in history that was innately evil; there is no moral relativity in genocide. Neither is there moral relativity with sickness, murder, or abuse. Yes, different contexts may provide more appropriate interpretations of each situation, but across all contexts, we find certain things to be unequivocally evil.

Furthermore, the problem of sin exists regardless of our interpretation of sin. The Christian and non-Christian may disagree about what constitutes evil, but different interpretations do not determine its absence or presence.

> You may have seen the bumper sticker that reads, "God said it! I believe it! That settles it!" But let's ask ourselves, "If God exists and communicates with human beings, then how does my believing it (or not) settle anything at all?" A more accurate rendering of this slogan would be, "God said it! That settles it whether I believe it or not!" We have to differentiate between the truth of a particular belief and the belief (or the act of believing) itself. For example, it's true that $2 + 2 = 4$. But this or that person may not believe that $2 + 2 = 4$.[5]

Just as Paul Copan addresses that $2 + 2 = 4$ regardless of whether someone disagrees or not, so sin is sin regardless of whether the Christian or non-Christian views it as such. And the Bible does a sufficient job of informing us of that which is sinful, regardless of our interpretations (Romans 1:28–32). However, these sinful acts are just a reflection of sinful beings, for 1 Corinthians 2:14 states, "The natural person does not accept the things of the Spirit of God, for they are folly to Him, and He is not able to understand them because they are spiritually discerned." We, apart from God, cannot accept what is right and godly because we are inherently sinful beings (because of the Fall in Genesis 3). When God saw the sin that was rampant in the world, He "gave [people] up in the lusts of their hearts to impurity, to the dishonoring of their bodies among themselves, because they exchanged the truth about God for a lie and worshiped and served the creature rather than the Creator" (Romans 1:24–25). Sin is inescapable apart from Christ. We are not evil in relation to the person who states we are evil; we are sinful because without God, we serve ourselves instead of Him.

Moral relativists may make this argument by claiming that their sins are only sins if they say they are sins, justifying their behavior to gratify their own lives, as if they do not belong to Someone else. However, if the problem defines the system, then God seeing us as sinful defines our state apart from Him. Without Christ, we are sinners with no hope of righteousness; we are moral relativists claiming sin is nonexistent while it eats our souls to death.

Our story does not end in death;
it begins with Jesus's life.

But our story does not end in death: "While we were still sinners, Christ died for us" (Romans 5:8). Christ died on our behalf to pay for the sin that depraved our hearts. Yet He did even more than die for us; He rose to life, defeating not only sin, but death as well. Sin has no dominion over Christ, and Paul tells us in Romans 6:14, "For sin will have no dominion over you, since you are not under law but under grace." Sin terrorized our souls, but Christ washed them to be purer than snow, gracing us in no humanly possible way. Our story does not end in death; it begins with Jesus's life.

Therefore, we are no longer defined by our past selves. If we were, then we would be riddled by guilt, shame, and sin. However, God gave us a new life in Christ; we were "born again to a living hope" (1 Peter 1:3). We do not have to live as though we are constrained by the flesh or by sin. Instead, we can live as though we are constrained by hope because hope lives in us by means of the Holy Spirit, which comes only through Jesus.

God's grace never runs out on us,
so we no longer have to insist on
living as if it does.

When we live in fear, guilt, or shame, we are not living as Christians who have abundant hope. Christ gives us the privilege of being strong enough to defeat the sin that threatens our hope because "everyone who has been born of God overcomes the world" (1 John 5:4). When Christ gives us a new life through the knowledge of His grace, we have a new life. And this new life is not futile; it is powerful enough to overcome any temptation that arises. We must stop living as though sin wins, because where sin abounds, grace abounds all the more (Romans 5:20). God's grace never runs out on us, so we no longer have to insist on living as if it does.

God may define sin as being apparent in the human heart, but He defines Christians as dead to that sin and alive to God (Romans 6:11). Therefore, God no longer defines us by the problem within the system. Instead, He defines us by the Solution of His Son, who saves us from the enslavement of sin forever.

To Sin or Not to Sin

When I was running around a new city with new friends before the accident, I was somewhat aware that my actions were not particularly glorifying to God. I elevated the image of myself and how others perceived me as more important in my heart than seeking to share the gospel with them. Even though I was not always technically engaging in sinful behavior, I was conscious of the fact that my character had shifted dramatically from one season of life to another.

We can reframe this conscious awareness as conviction. The Christian community associates the word *conviction* with God, making us aware of our sin through the Holy Spirit. The Spirit convicts through our conscience, bringing light to sin that we would otherwise ignore. Even though I was repeating sinful patterns, God convicted me when I felt shame for some of my dishonoring actions. The Spirit worked on my conscience throughout that time, wearing down my desire to please others and myself and increasing my desire to please God first and foremost.

The Spirit convicting us is a form of spiritual discipline. Although many people may shy away from the word *discipline*, it is actually more positive than negative. Discipline brings us closer to righteousness and gives us a fuller picture of God's goodness, so discipline is far from undesirable.

God disciplines us because we are His children; but unlike our earthly fathers, God disciplines us perfectly.[6] If you're like me, you have probably felt the failings of earthly dads. I, for one, did not even meet my biological father until I was a senior in high school, and I have only seen him twice since. I also witnessed the man whom I claimed as my dad (my sister's dad) divorce my mom and leave me in the dust. No dad on this earth will measure up to God because no earthly father is perfect. But we can offer grace to them because God has offered grace to us. God's discipline is not punishment because Jesus received all punishment for us.[7] Take a moment and let that sink in: any discipline from God is *not* punishment for our sins. We do not have to feel guilt or shame or fear.

When considering whether or not to participate in sin (thoughts, actions, or conversations), we can depend on the Bible and our consciences to lead us in the most God-honoring direction. The Bible is clear on many things that displease God, but many people try to slide into a gray area of sin that is not explicitly stated in the Bible. However, the Spirit also gives us the Holy Spirit to work on our consciences to make the less clear sins more apparent (Romans 2:15). Our conscience functions in our heart in a way similar to how pain functions in the body: When we obey our conscience, we have peace; when we disobey, we have pain.[8]

Thus, when we do not have peace, we can know that our conscience is revealing disobedience to God's Word. When we strive to uphold a life that glorifies God, we can work hard "to have a clear conscience toward both God and man" (Acts 24:16). As Martin Luther said, "My conscience is captive to the Word of God."[9] Not only should we recognize a discontented conscience and clear it up to be one of peace, but we should desire for that conscience to be captivated by God's Word. When we lean on truth rather than uncertainty of the gray areas of sin, we will, in turn, love God and people more like Christ. [10]

> *The aim of our charge is love that issues from a pure heart and a good conscience and a sincere faith.*
>
> 1 Timothy 1:5

Therefore, although sin is in this world, we can lean on the gospel truth that Jesus has paid for our sin. Jesus is immanent and inherent in our identity as cleansed children of God. We no longer have to long after other water bottles; we have the Water of Life within reach because Jesus made a way to our hearts. We no longer have to place other loves before Him and feel the weight of their disappointments; we have freedom to choose God because Jesus chose us first. And finally, we can relax under the rest that comes with a clear conscience of placing our lives in Jesus's hands.

Reflect:

- ☐ What goals do you have?
- ☐ What about meeting those goals is important to you?
- ☐ What or who are your disordered loves?

Practice:

- ☐ Think about a few of your choices today (or yesterday if you're reading this in the morning). Write them down and then evaluate them in light of God's Word. How could you have responded biblically? How will you respond moving forward?

Chapter Three
Under the Influence

I returned to work after a week of recovery. But with the return to work came the return to driving. Even though the thought of getting behind the wheel spooked me, I did not want fear to rule over me. I refused to let worry cripple me from living my life.

I drove to and from work for several weeks, slowly confronting my fears.

However, one day, the fear overtook me in a way I had not expected.

Brake lights blinked red ahead, and I gently pumped my own brakes. The cars around me sped past as I allowed plenty of distance between my car and the car in front. I grimaced as cars whipped by—too quickly, in my opinion.

But soon, we were all inching along, our vehicles halted by some commotion up ahead. I did not want to see it. Passing by even the smallest of accidents since my family's wreck caused me—someone who had once claimed to be almost fearless—to go in a state of panic.

This drive home had become routine for me over the past month and a half. But we were getting closer to the place on the freeway where many cars had to merge on a short stretch of road. When I first moved to the city, driving this stretch of road made me nervous. The combination of two on-ramps and two exit-only lanes on a speedy highway called for heightened awareness. The stretch had been scary initially, but I had quickly overcome any fear so I could think more clearly and make safer decisions. But as the other drivers and I continued edging closer to that section of highway, the same fear crept back into my chest.

The middle-of-the-afternoon traffic was certainly better than at rush hour, but we still had to move into the left lanes. As I got closer, I realized we all had to squeeze into only the far left lane, leaving four empty lanes.

Empty, that is, except for the wreck.

When I saw the 18-wheeler, my palms began to sweat.

But it was seeing the white Jeep that made my head spin. The Jeep was underneath and in front of the back wheels of the 18-wheeler—crushed. Emergency responders were struggling to get someone out. Right before my eyes, I saw the horror of the wreck—the same fear I so vividly remembered from only weeks before.

Tears fell from my eyes, and my breathing felt heavy and hard. I prayed out loud and in my head over the whole situation, remembering the fervent prayers of the stranger who had prayed over me while I was lying on the side of the road. I half wanted to pull over and pray, but I knew too well the hectic manner of those moments. The last thing I wanted to do was get in the way of someone's life or death.

But God knew and heard my prayers. Although I will never know if the person or people in that white Jeep survived, I can trust that God at least helped me get through that stretch. I was hardly able to see from the dizziness of the panic, but God kept my vehicle straight on the highway, unscathed physically from the horrific scene.

It may appear that I simply discovered the accident as I rounded the corner, but more than merely discovering it, I actually participated in the process of inventing it.[1] I'm not saying I imagined it; the accident involving a white Jeep happened, and I was a witness to it. But as constructive beings, we construct the world around us through our senses and perceptions rather than external objects filling in our world independent of our participation. Therefore, we do not discover as though uninvolved in the world around us; instead, our brains fill in our surroundings because we participate in our surroundings. We are just as much part of the constructive process as those around us, making us all inventors of reality because we all influence reality.

So far, we have analyzed how God is the only One who could be inside and outside our system. He is not only part of the system, but He created the system. Therefore, God invented everything when He created the universe. (And who knows what else He could have invented before the origins of the universe?) He did not discover the world as though it were there before He could discover it—He was the first inventor.

Therefore, since God created us in His image, we can use the creativity established by God to create the world in which we live. Our creation may look different from God's invention, but we invent nonetheless, as John MacArthur stated,

> Worldly wisdom can't know God through the study of objective facts and it can't know Him internally through a subjective thought process. The world is in a hopeless state but God has a great plan. The secret to knowing God is loving Him through Jesus Christ. The human mind does not discover God. God revealed Himself to the human mind in Christ.[2]

Just as we cannot discover a completely holy God out of our completely sinful nature, we cannot discover reality without the One who invented reality. And if the Inventor of reality did not discover it, then how would a participant of the reality outside of the system discover it? We, as part of the universal system, influence and therefore invent the reality in which we live.

We all have constructed the world around us based on our senses. Those of us who have sight have processed from birth the shadows, lights, and colors around us so our realities make sense. Our brains automatically learn how to account for the world around us by using our senses. However, unlike many postmodern thinkers, I do not hold this philosophy to be completely true for everything, or I would find myself inevitably in contradiction. Copan addresses this problem:

> The person who believes reality is like a wet lump of clay says something self-contradictory or just trivial.

He either believes his view is a universal reality, or it is just something he himself has created, which means it does not apply to others. . . . [So] we can ask him, "Is your idea—that each of us can shape our own reality—nothing more than a reality you yourself created? Is this wet-lump-of-clay idea something you invented? If so, why do you think it applies to me at all?" Of course, our friend certainly appears to be saying that his view *does* apply to everyone. In that case, he has contradicted himself. He ultimately believes that not *all* reality can be created. Some things are real or exist, about which we can do absolutely nothing.[3]

I particularly appreciate Copan's comments because his point ultimately directs us back to the One who creates all reality. Although we have influence, we have no power over God's authority within His realm of which we have no knowledge or control. Therefore, although we invent and have influence in our reality, we have no power over God. He rules and reigns in perfect authority. This reality gives us freedom and empowerment both to create a better reality and to trust in a completely good God who is working all things together exactly as He has planned.

We have power over our reality to invent good and create an environment that is conducive to living a godly life.

When encountering belief systems, some people may claim, "I'll believe it when I see it." This statement resounds with what Heinz von Foerster (a scientist I discovered in grad school) talked about when he referred to the saying "seeing is believing."[4] Thus, what we see is what we believe to be true based on our perceptions. When we see good happening, we believe good is happening. When we see bad happening, we believe bad is happening. Therefore, rather than filling our sight and vision with negative realities, we can fill our line of sight with good. We have power over our reality to invent good and create an environment that is conducive to living a godly life. We are not outside reality or unable to influence it. We all have influence on each other, which means we all have influence on and in our realities.

In fact, we can close our perceptions to that which detracts from living a life focused on Christ. Although we can certainly be aware of the world around us—even the parts of the world that do not glorify Christ—we can focus on Christ and Christ alone. Doing so helps us see what glorifies God so we don't focus on what doesn't glorify God. We may know sin exists, but we do not participate in it. We live lives of honor rather than lives of horror.

Therefore, we can use our power of invention over reality to construct a life pleasing to God. And when we participate in thinking, behaving, and living in line with a sense of self that God declares over us, we find strength in the stability of the unchanging perspective of the First Inventor of reality.

Under Construction

Understanding the construction process allows us to be more aware of what we process.[5] More importantly, *knowing* how we process reality lends us the opportunity to *alter* how we process reality.

Before I researched PTSD (post-traumatic stress disorder), I was unaware of why I was processing car accidents in such a way. Of course, I knew that my heightened awareness of traumatic scenes was a direct result of my own wreck, but I was not sure how to control the physical and emotional responses that arose every time I passed even the mildest accident scenes.

However, once I became more aware of how those with PTSD process traumatic scenes, I began to change how I processed seeing accidents. After meeting once with a campus counselor to confirm my experience, I made some changes. First, I created a playlist on Spotify to listen to while driving, and I labeled it "praise>ptsd." Because I have an organizational type of personality, I enjoyed the process of inserting uplifting music into a playlist. I also was intentional about the music on the playlist; I did not include music that would dampen my mood but only music that praised God. This decision arose from my solution-focused therapy training, for I wanted to focus my mind on what would be helpful rather than harmful. I knew that I could praise God through music and focus on my blessings and my Blesser rather than focus on accidents I might pass on the highway.

Then I chose to rely more on Jesus than myself. I acted on that reliance by being intentional about my time reading

Scripture and by journaling more frequently. Rather than reading Scripture as part of routine, I read Scripture in light of its context and meaning to go beyond surface-level application. By focusing on that, I could understand God's Word more clearly, which led to my enjoying God much more.

In finding joy in God and listening to music that praised Him, I found that my language began to change. Instead of complaining about my experiences, I began to praise God for giving me new experiences every time I woke up to a new day. After I developed an understanding of how I was processing trauma, I could change how I processed that trauma so I could live a life more glorifying to God.

This concept extends beyond trauma. We process millions of images daily, whether we realize it or not. Regarding identity, we process many messages of the world that demand our attention. Rather than listening to lies from the world, we can choose to see the world in light of who God is. The world is sinful and leads us astray, but God will never lead us astray.

> *Do not love the world or the things in the world. If anyone loves the world, the love of the Father is not in him. For all that is in the world—the desires of the flesh and the desires of the eyes and pride of life—is not from the Father but is from the world. <u>And the world is passing away along with its desires, but whoever does the will of God abides forever.</u>*
>
> 1 John 2:15–17; emphasis added

Knowing that we process reality by what we focus on

allows us to focus on focusing. Although we are part of the world and know that sin and the world exist (like the dark spot in the image), we can focus on what is good and pleasing to God (like the star), which will limit the world's power over our vision of our lives.

To Observe

As I passed the white Jeep crushed beneath the 18-wheeler, I didn't know how the incident occurred. I didn't know the people in the accident, nor did I know the people in the many vehicles trying to squeeze into the one left lane. I was outside of the situation.

Or so it would seem.

However, we are "observing systems, not observed systems; we cannot attain a 'God's eye view.'"[6] Perhaps one might analyze this statement by saying the "system" includes all those affected by the accident. Upon first thought, those affected might seem to include only those injured in their wrecked vehicles. However, are not the first responders also affected by the incident? And what about their families? Say a first responder was late getting home for dinner because of the accident; who knows how that affected his or her family. Furthermore, onlookers like me also experienced the effects of the wreck, for we all had to slow down our usual speed during that stretch of highway. And slowing down was only one way the accident affected onlookers. As I mentioned earlier, the wreck also emotionally, mentally, and physically influenced me, so I called my mom. Now, a year later, I am writing about it. So when does the "system" end? This question leads to the necessary step of tossing out any concept of humans escaping influence, so we cannot observe a system as though we are not part of it.

As Humberto Maturana and Francisco Varela taught, we cannot attain a "God's-eye view" of the world.[7] We are not omniscient beings; therefore, we cannot observe the world as though the world does not influence us and as though we do not influence the world. We, as temporal beings in a fleeting world, do not know the system as it actually is because we are part of the system, which therefore subjects us to influence. This certainty is inescapable. Only God can have a "God's-eye view." We cannot obtain the level of objectivity that God has, but we can justify that His objectivity is the only objectivity that we can trust.

> Although we must acknowledge our limitations, biases, and perspectives, we are not doomed by our environment to mere "perspective." Some measure of objectivity is possible. . . . There is at least *some* objective reality that applies to everyone and that cannot be altered by us. We are not being "arrogant" or "imperialistic," therefore, if we assert that *some* aspect of reality cannot be manipulated by human thought or action. If a person strongly disagrees with us, he will presumably do so on the basis of a reality he thinks applies to both parties! So even if a person is incorrect about what is actually real, everyone inescapably believes that some kind of objective reality exists. This being

so, the discussion can move beyond the question, "Does objective reality exist?" to, "Given that objective reality is unavoidable, how do I justify or support my understanding of objective reality?"[8]

When we realize that we are intricately connected in an infinite number of ways, we can find both comfort in community and awe for our Creator.

When we realize that we are intricately connected in an infinite number of ways, we can find both comfort in community and awe for our Creator. Realizing our own places as necessary elements in God's will produces a spirit of worship. God exists within our system and outside our system—a fact that in itself is inescapably amazing. We, in our limited scope, cannot account for such a concept, yet God can. Because He is omniscient and omnipotent, His character is trustworthy.

Consequently, rather than living as though we are not part of God's system—as though we are above the influence of any creature—we have the power to live in synchrony as participants in the system. This reality allows us to relax, and the beauty of having such an amazing God is that He not only influenced the universe into creation, He sent Jesus to earth to restore a fallen world to Himself. We have the ability to constantly communicate with God through both His Word and the Holy Spirit. God has the power to be deistic (outside His creation), but He also chooses to be theistic (connected with His creation). Although He may have the ability to be separate, for He is above and over time and His creation, He chooses to influence our lives in ways we cannot begin to fathom.

Once we grapple with this reality, we can come to an understanding that we are not only important enough for God to create us as influential, but we are also important enough for God to choose to influence us. God wants to use us for His purpose and plan, and what better way to thank the God of the universe than to serve Him and place our entire identities in Him.

Reflect:

- ☐ What are a few Bible verses that remind you of God's sovereignty?
- ☐ How do you trust God when all else fails?
- ☐ How do you stay mindful of Him when life is good?

Practice:

- ☐ Picture yourself as perfectly secure in your identity. Think of at least 10 things about yourself that would indicate to you that you are perfectly secure. Write them down somewhere important. You don't even have to think about what you have to do to get there. Just get an idea of what "perfectly secure" means.

Chapter Four
From Screamo to Sorority Girl

A stigma lies within our culture, taking root in our hearts and causing us to portray what is not real. Many people associate it with church people or rich people, but this way of life is prevalent across all socioeconomic, religious, and social strata.

We are all guilty of being, or appearing, fake.

Long before the accident, when I was in high school, I resisted the notion that I, of all people, was fake. I did not like the cheerleader type, nor did I like the happy, popular type; I stereotyped all of them as fake. So I spent my high school years being "real" with my emotions, which meant talking about the deeper things in life, missing the fleeting pleasures of high school culture, and judging others daily.

One summer evening before I went off to college, my stepdad asked me if I was going to rush a sorority. I literally guffawed and thought he might have lost his mind. Me? The girl who wore sweatpants and T-shirts with punk-rock-band-autographed Converse shoes and had a distaste for spending time with girls? I had assumed he was just joking, which was typical of his lighthearted personality.

But God sure has a funny way of working.

He showed me that every person has a story and that each person's story matters to Him, so they should matter to me.

In college, I noticed that not everyone was fake. I saw young women gathering and having fun while pouring out their lives for Christ. God changed my heart and showed me the value of surrounding myself with other believers who were women. He showed me that every person has a story and that each person's story matters to Him, so they should matter to me. He revealed to me the sweet fellowship that happens when women gather without comparing themselves to each other, without judging one another, and without the ugly stereotypes I had built in my heart.

Most importantly, He revealed to me how sinful I had been in high school, where I had judged others without even knowing anything about their lives. But who was I to judge anyone (Romans 14:4)? I had participated in the very hypocrisy that I had despised in others, and as I learned the depth of my own sin, God also started working in my heart.

Much to my surprise, I made my way up the ranks of leadership in a sorority and loved every minute of it. What was different about the sororities at my private university was that they were all Christ-centered, which was a blossoming concept to me at the time. One thing I always sought to do was be real with the girls in the sorority, trying to portray the value of being genuine to each woman I encountered. The last thing I wanted to do as a recovering judge-aholic was to make anyone feel judged or inferior in a place where I wanted them to feel welcome and safe.

But after I graduated and left the sorority, I hid behind a mask of Christianity while I participated in sinful activities. I went to church just as regularly as I had before, but something changed when I turned 21. Others' perceptions of me became so much more important as I reestablished myself in a new environment. I had flourished in my undergraduate university, for it had become familiar and comfortable. However, whenever I found myself in an unfamiliar place that was uncomfortable for my Christian walk, I stumbled.

Something changed in those couple of months between finishing my undergraduate program and starting graduate school, long before the accident.

My sorority had been a huge part of my undergraduate life. I devoted most of my free time to leading and meeting with the girls involved. I surrounded myself with godly people, and I loved it. After I graduated, however, I moved away from campus and began a new life. I went from being a sorority vice president who led all our members to being just another member of society. No longer were people looking to me for guidance. No longer were people holding me accountable. And no longer was there a community of believers who understood the same struggles I wrestled with, especially regarding my identity.

I was alone again.

So I clung to the first thing that came along: men. I tried to fill the new void of attention by seeking guys' approval, but I always found myself barren and in need of more. This emptiness epitomizes the flaw of needing approval from people. Their affirmation may sound pleasant at the time, but we will always need more. I grasped at any amount of attention I could receive—both during my undergraduate years and after—rather than finding satisfaction in the attention that God had so graciously given me. And as a result, my satisfaction came up short.

No one would have known this struggle lurked beneath the surface of my bubbly laughter. In high school, I despised girls who appeared perfect, but after graduation, I became the very person I had once judged so harshly.

Christians and non-Christians both place such a high value on perception, and perception drives a portion of how we construct our own sense of self. We may perceive others as living flawless lives and think we have to be flawless, too, or we may perceive others as sinning repeatedly and think falling into such behavior is acceptable. My hope is that instead, we perceive ourselves in light of who God is and offer the same grace that He offers to all of us.

Actively Perceiving

"Per-ception is much closer to an act of creation, as in con-ception, than to a passive state of affairs, as in re-ception."[1] I love this quote from von Foerster because it reverses the norms of our present culture. He places the value on the one who is doing the perceiving rather than the perceived. Whenever we recognize our surroundings, we actively participate in what we see. Rather than receiving our surroundings passively, we automatically focus more on some things than others.

As we go about our days, certain images catch our eye, whereas other messages fall outside our perception. And what one perceives says more about the perceiver than it ever will about the perceived.[2]

For example, if I am driving on a highway, I may notice a billboard that advertises something about Jesus. I can think of two that I've seen lately: exploreGod.com and the one that says "7 days without prayer makes one weak." Although I may recognize these billboards because I have an interest in Jesus, agnostics who do not care about whether or not God exists may be completely unaware of the billboards. Neither the agnostic's nor my noticing the billboards affects who God is, nor does our viewing of the billboard change the realities of those who own the billboards. What these billboards do, however, is highlight what is or is not important in our own hearts.

Taking this billboard example further, I also would venture to say that my perception was more conception because I take in what I want to take in. I create my reality by fusing together the images I want to see to formulate my surroundings. Although I would not take this theory so far as to say I physically alter anything through perception, I do mentally create my reality through the act of perceiving my environment. I see what I want to see and do not see what I may not want to see.

This, of course, may be true most of the time, but we also are subject to others' perceptions and actions as they impede upon our realities. Therefore, no matter how much we create a world we would want to see, we still have millions of other people who are doing the same, which will inevitably result in people seeing what they do not want to see as well. This idea only goes so far, but the power of perception still stands, especially as it relates to who we are in Christ.

Thus, if the act of perceiving says more about the perceiver than the perceived, then we can view God and perception in two different ways.

Man Perceives God

The more we look to God, the more we find how unholy we are in comparison. However, everything in the universe is meant to worship God, which says way more about how great God is than how terrible we are. Pictures of Jesus's loving relationship toward us are all just a shadow of what is to come (Revelation 21). Our suffering and our sin will not get the last laugh.[3]

Whenever we look to God and see how great He is, we know that God is restoring our sinful lives to look more like Jesus. And we know that because the whole universe is Jesus's temple, God is restoring the physical as well as the spiritual.[4]

No distinction is apparent. God cares about our souls; and going even further, matter matters to God.

C. S. Lewis discusses matter in the art of perception:

> Matter, which keeps souls apart, also brings them together. It enables each of us to have an "outside" as well as an "inside," so that what are acts of will and thought for you are noises and glances for me; you are enabled not only to *be*, but to *appear* and hence I have the pleasure of making your acquaintance.[5]

God uses matter in ways that we could not even imagine. Lewis mentions matter in the sense of each person being individual (inside/thoughts) and also social (outside/will). Furthermore, when we translate the internal into the external in a social environment, the matter that makes us up becomes perceivable to another. Without matter, perception would be impossible because there would be nothing to perceive. Matter matters to God and matters to us.[6] Therefore, we create our perceptions out of the matter that both we and the perceived exert.

As a result, the more we perceive God in our daily lives, the more we will see His influence on us. As we look to Him more, we will begin to look like Him more. Because perception says more about the perceiver than the perceived, the more we perceive God, the more we will look like Him. However, as we see this result, we must not neglect the utmost importance of how God perceives us, which shows His endless love for us.

God Perceives Man

As Christians, God sees us as holy and blameless because of Jesus (Ephesians 1:4). What does that say about God? If we are holy and blameless in His sight because of Jesus, regardless of our depraved state and continual turn to sin, then we find that God is so gracious that He overflows with holiness and blamelessness unto us. We find at least six points in the Bible that point to how God sees us.

First, God sees us as members of His household (Ephesians 2:19). This analogy shows us that God holds family in high honor and is relational. God is not raising His children (us) in isolation from Him as though deistic. He is One in Three Persons and includes all Christians in His household as a welcoming, caring, and perfect Father.

Second, God sees us as justified for all our sins (Romans 5:1). Because He finds us as justified, we know that our God is just. And even though the justice we deserved was death, Jesus suffered the penalty for all our sins. God administered justice to the point of His Son's death on a cross, so we can trust that He will be just both now and forevermore.

Third, God sees us as new creations (2 Corinthians 5:17). Therefore, we know that God wants to see redemption fulfilled. He does not desire Christians to resort to old habits of sin, but He desires us to live the new life He has given us, because in Him is newness of life. God, the Giver of Life, has given new life abundantly to us because of His gracious nature.

Fourth, God has healed us from sin (1 Peter 2:24). His seeing us as healed shows us how great of a healer He is. No doctor or nurse or therapist could compare to the healing that God does every second of our lives.

Fifth, God sees us as the righteousness of God (2 Corinthians 5:21). Because Jesus took on all our sin, God does not see us for the filth that crippled us in the past. Instead, He sees us as righteous, which reveals how much more righteous He is.

Sixth, and finally, God sees us as the light of the world (Matthew 5:14) because He is the light of the world. In a world fallen into sin and darkness, God brought light through Jesus Christ. Without Him, we would be blinded by darkness and sin, but with Him, the light is on, and we can see a glimmer of how bright and good He is.

Creatively Creating

God has created us with a creative spirit, which matches the idea that perception is a creative process. I would not go so far as to say we can simply think things into being (for only the Creator could invent matter with a single thought or word). But I would say that we have a spark of creativity connected to our sense of perception because the One in whose image we were made has more creativity than we could ever fathom.

I have already discussed the art of conceiving a perception, but now I want to discuss the creativity behind the conception. Our culture currently promotes individualism and original creation, and we can certainly find some originality in how God created us.

God was the first creative being. He was the first to invent something from scratch and create something out of an idea. He also created us in His image, so when we find ourselves using creativity and originality, we know that it is because we are children of God. When God created Eve, He used His conception of Adam to create a woman, who was like him in species but different in many ways. Thus, His perception of the woman was a creative process.

Furthermore, when Adam took in his wife's beauty for the first time, he was certainly creative with his words. He did not passively receive her but actively participated in perceiving her as part of his creative thinking, which he portrayed with words of admiration (Genesis 2:23).

We also know that perception is involvement of both the perceiver and the perceived. Therefore, we can use our creativity in the perception process to perceive what will bring us closer to Jesus. Rather than creatively going to an unseemly bar and perceiving a dark environment, which could lead us astray, we can creatively go to a calmer place where we can perceive a more relaxed environment for conversations about Jesus.

Creativity is fun, and following Jesus is fun, despite society's attacks on the definition of "fun." Fun should involve honoring God rather than seeking pleasure at any cost. We must honor Him because of all that He has done for and continues to do for us. As sinners in constant need of sanctification, we must serve our God with everything in us to make His grace all the more known.

We can look at the creative process of perception

by also looking at the transcendence, immanence, and providence of God. God's transcendence is His presence beyond the here and now. His immanence is God's inherent presence in the here and now. And His providence is His good sovereignty over His creation. All these concepts are true of God's character, but what do these character traits reveal about who we are in light of Him?[7]

We better understand these concepts if we look at them backward. Rather than trying to understand transcendence and immanence first, we can look at the outcome of the two, which is God's providence. As we develop a better understanding of God's providence, we also will develop a better understanding of His transcendence and immanence.

First, providence is always about the person giving the providence, not about the person being used to reveal providence. Thus, when God showed His sovereignty by changing my heart and leading me to godly community in my sorority, I did not exclaim how great I was for finding provision. Instead, I proclaimed how great God was because of His intervention. His providence in my life was not a means to glorify me; instead, it returned the glory to Him.

These incidents thus revealed God's immanence in my life. If He were a deistic God (distant and uninvolved), He would not know my needs and would never intervene when I needed His help. However, His continual provision for me shows that He is not a distant God. He is immanent in my life and in my heart, calling me every day to depend more on Him and less on me.

> *Because I know that I can trust Him based on His continual provision over me, I know I will always be able to trust Him to provide in the future.*

This leads to my understanding of God's transcendence, for my dependence on His providence and immanence shows His knowledge of what I need before I need it. This awareness goes beyond my present situations and into future occurrences. Because I know that I can trust Him based on His continual provision over me, I know that I will always be able to trust Him to provide in the future. His sovereignty is not only in the past and present but also extends into the future, beyond anything I can imagine, therefore portraying His transcendence.

The art of perception can go many ways. In the above example, I could have perceived God as any of the three attributes and enjoyed learning more about God's character on all three levels. However, rather than stopping at only one incidence of perception, I can create a reality that includes a more holistic view of God. God does not limit our perception to only one way of viewing the world; He gives us many avenues of analyzing circumstances to reveal more and more of His own character.

Rather than resting in laziness, we need to grow in our own faith by pursuing creativity through actively creating perceptions that glorify God over self.

Simply being aware of the endless possibilities of upholding a creative approach to perception can open our eyes to seeing even more of God's constant influence in our lives. Why limit ourselves to one perception when we can create much deeper realities that will point our lives to Jesus even more? Many people have testified to God's good character by telling amazing stories of His grace. We must never grow satisfied with a view that limits God; instead, we must always pursue deeper insights of God's unfathomably incredible character by understanding the many facets of God. Rather than resting in laziness, we need to grow in our own faith by pursuing creativity through actively creating perceptions that glorify God over self.

Responding with Responsibility

Perception may be a powerful part of what we introduce into our realities, but as we become more aware of how much our own minds create the reality in which we live, we also must accept the responsibility that comes with it. Responsibility comes from acceptance that perception is each individual's creation.[8]

As I transitioned from my high school way of thinking

to a more gospel-centered way of thinking, my perceptions began to change. Before, my perceptions of blonde, skinny women who wore the sorority costume made me grimace, causing hateful judgments and comparative thoughts. As a direct result of my judgment-filled heart, I perceived pretty girls as fake.

Once I started seeing other girls as human beings with souls God cares for, I began to see how flawed I was. Not only had I been elevating myself above them, but I also had been elevating myself over God.

Once I started seeing other girls as human beings with souls God cares for, I began to see how flawed I was. Not only had I been elevating myself above them, but I also had been elevating myself over God.

We are all flawed (Romans 3), but I had assumed that other women's flaws were graver than my own. But God did not send Jesus to die for only some of His people's sins. He died for all of His people's sins. No sin is greater than another; we all fall short, and Jesus died for sin, regardless of its nature.

Everyone has something to overcome. This life is not easy, and a sinful world is going to include pain. No one escapes life without some sort of obstacle or difficulty. Regardless of how intense the obstacle is to an outsider, the one experiencing a trial still has to figure out how to overcome that trial. Rather than assuming sorority girls did not have stories of struggle, I began to see them as strong and able. Not only did they defeat hard times, but they did so with joy and confidence, which I had not yet learned to do.

My sorority dedicated time out of our weekly meetings to giving women chances to share their testimonies. As each woman shared stories of pain, hardship, and triumph because of Jesus, I grew less callous and more aware of God's work among them. My perception then changed to one of respect and admiration. God does not limit His work to non-sorority girls who are supposedly real; He works His sovereign hand through all people to accomplish His will. How naïve and judgmental I was to limit God's power and judge His children in the process.

As Christians, we have a responsibility over our perceptions to uphold a reality that is true. Rather than leaning on worldly understandings of our surroundings, we must cling to God's Word for guidance. Rather than judging others, we can rely on the fact that judgment belongs to Jesus alone (John 5:22). Rather than conforming to the ways of the world, we can allow Jesus to transform our lives to look more gracious and loving (Romans 12:2). Rather than having minds that are of the world, we can have the mind of Christ (1 Corinthians 2:16; Philippians 2:5).

These few examples of gospel-centered thinking will result in gospel-centered perceptions. If perception is what reveals our own hearts, then we must be diligent in guiding our perceptions. That means we have to examine our hearts

(2 Corinthians 13:5). We must remove the plank from our own eye (Matthew 7:5) so we may see God's workmanship (Ephesians 2:10). May we take responsibility for our perceptions and eliminate the sin that prevents us from seeing God's goodness in and among His people.

Reflection:

- ☐ What truths from the Bible help you when Satan tempts you to believe lies?
- ☐ How does God influence you?
- ☐ How do you block out influences that steal your joy?

Practice:

- ☐ Get out a piece of paper and a writing utensil. Think of that "perfectly secure" future self that you imagined in the last chapter. Now, pretend you are that self, and write a letter to your current self. What advice would your future self give your current self to overcome your current struggles? Include specifics. Your letter can be as long or as short as you like.

Part Two
Thinking Out Loud

Chapter Five
By Word of Mouth

I couldn't see anything clearly at the hospital. Losing my contact lens in the accident rendered me almost blind, and I didn't have my backup eyeglasses with me. During this time, I relied on others' voices to understand my situation.

The Use of Words

During my hospital stay and on the trip back to Texas, my social reality was the essence of my reality for quite some time. Whenever I spoke, I used words to formulate my thoughts, feelings, and meanings, primarily because I could not use my sense of sight. Even when I finally returned home to a new pair of eyeglasses, I continued to rely on verbiage to communicate. Regardless of how we use words, we attempt to understand each other using mainly words. Non-verbal signals may also play a vital role in communication, but we mainly default to words because exchanging words is a natural process that flows from our social nature.

This natural use of words flows out of an innate sense

of sociality that comes from God. Genesis shows us that God used words to create, similar in a sense to how we use words to create meaning. He spoke things into being and called them by name. God created by speaking— by using His words. Therefore, in thinking of identity and who we are in light of who God is, we can know that speaking and using words plays an important role.

And God said, "Let there be light," and there was light. And God saw that the light was good. And God separated the light from the darkness. God called the light Day, and the darkness he called Night. And there was evening and there was morning, the first day.

Genesis 1:3–5

The words in this passage have a couple of distinct perspectives. One perspective suggests that God uses His words to define, and He does put definitions to His words here. However, another perspective offers that God *uses* words to *describe* their uses. He used the word *day* to describe the light, and He used the word *night* to describe darkness. He did not define the two by explaining how many hours, seconds, and nanoseconds are in each portion of the day or night (although I am sure He knew how many hours, seconds, and nanoseconds would be in each one). Instead of defining, He simply *used* words both to create day and night and to provide us with an understanding of how He described the light and the darkness so that we, too, can use His words in describing His creation.

Another way to view this phenomenon is to look at God's reasons for creating language in the first place, otherwise known as the Tripartite View of Language.[1] The basic premise is this: God used words to create language so He could communicate with people. He also created language in order for people to communicate with God. Finally, He created language so people could communicate with other people. God used words as part of forming a bridge to how we understand each other.

C. S. Lewis describes this concept in *Mere Christianity* as it relates particularly to the labeling of Christians and non-Christians.

> In the first place, Christians themselves will never be able to apply it [the label "Christian"] to anyone. . . . It would be wicked arrogance for us to say that any man is, or is not, a Christian in this refined sense. . . . *It is only a question of using words so that we can all understand what is being said* (emphasis added).[2]

Lewis addresses the core concept of how God uses words. Similarly, we use words to understand each other; we do not constantly define words for the sake of defining them. Definitions are too definitive (or too absolute) for subjective beings such as ourselves. Besides, what would be the use in definitions if we did not use them to understand each other?

Jesus also hits on the usefulness of words:

So Jesus said to the Jews who had believed him, "If you abide in my word, you are truly my disciples, and you will know the truth, and the truth will set you free."

John 8:31–32

Jesus instructs us to abide in truth—the Word of God or the Word that God uses to communicate with us. We are free from the slavery of sin once we recognize our place as sons and daughters of the King, and we know this through reading God's Word. God uses His Word to relay the truth of the gospel to us. Rather than toying with the idea of something as useless as debating over definitions (for each person brings a different history to the meaning of certain words), we as Christians should recognize what God wants to do *through* His Word and then pursue Him through His Word. And when we do, His Word will most certainly not turn up empty (Isaiah 55:11).

Each speaking person uses words regularly, naturally. But as we desire identities founded on truth rather than lies, we also must be aware of what proceeds from our mouths. Luke 6:45 instructs us that "out of the abundance of the heart his mouth speaks." Therefore, using our words for bitterness is a prime indication that our hearts are bitter. Likewise, if our hearts are finding joy in Jesus, then our words will reflect joy. We can use our words to recognize the state of our hearts.

Knowing that our joy and foundation rests in Someone who will always trump others' opinions frees us up to use our words for Him and no one else.

Words—both ours and others'—shape our identity. In finding an identity in Jesus, our words will reflect holiness, and others' words about us will do the same. And if others ever use their words to tear down our identity in Jesus, then we can lean on the stronger foundation of Jesus to bring something good out of their ill intents. Knowing that our joy and foundation rests in Someone who will always trump others' opinions frees us up to use our words for Him and no one else.

Girls' Night

The lights were low, the night was dark, and my roommate and I were watching *50 First Dates*, a 1990s comedy I had seen a handful of times before the wreck. We both snuggled into our separate plush blankets, each in her own place on her usual couch. She had her usual chocolate ice cream, and I had my Cherry Garcia. The pizza was already beginning to digest in our stomachs as we settled in for the rest of the evening. We were doing girls' night the way every girls' night should be done.

The evening took a turn for the worse, however, when the movie played back the event that caused the woman to lose her short-term memory. In just a few moments, I went from enjoying the funny movie to cringing away from the screen and burying my face in the blanket. I had not expected the replay of her car accident to affect me so much. My body shook, and I had to work to keep my breathing even. Before long, the movie was on pause, and my roommate and I were talking about PTSD.

Before that conversation, I had heard of PTSD being a possibility after traumatic accidents, but I never believed it would be true for me. Even though I had taken psychology classes, I had always considered PTSD as something only soldiers and veterans experienced upon returning from warfare. However, PTSD can affect anyone who has experienced something traumatic, whether it is military combat, car accidents, or abuse (to name only a few).

During our conversation, my roommate shared resources I had never heard of. And as I spoke of my experiences with anxiety and sadness, my experience seemed to become more real—more in sync with the symptoms of PTSD.

I might not have learned of these resources or understood the psychological distress that rose to the surface had my roommate and I not had this discussion. We equally participated in the discussion and thus equally shared in co-creating the social reality of our setting.[3] Through our conversation, my roommate and I created a social environment that was open, vulnerable, and helpful. We would not have come to this conclusion had we not had our conversation. Conversations influence us much more than we often realize.

Jesus exemplified the co-construction of social realities when He healed the woman who had been bleeding for 12 years. She merely touched His garment, having faith He would heal her without even speaking to Him, but Jesus responded using language. He knew the woman's thoughts even when she did not verbalize them, just as He knows our thoughts and our hearts (Psalm 139: 2, 4). The woman participated in co-creating her social reality simply by believing Jesus would heal her. And He responded with words since she could not know His thoughts: "Daughter, your faith has made you well; go in peace, and be healed of your disease" (Mark 5:34).

Since we cannot know the thoughts or experiences of another, we communicate through conversation to develop a social reality. Our social reality is just another facet of how we perceive identity.

So we are social beings, for God (who is social) created us in His image. Although sin permeated our world only chapters after humanity's story began, people still have an innate sense of being relational; sin did not take away the fact that God created us in His image to be interactional. Therefore, our social realities are still crucial in the formation of identity.

Thus, participating in conversations that reflect Jesus will support a preferred social reality founded on Jesus.

Thus, the content and those who participate in those conversations are both core elements of producing a more stable social reality and identity. Conversations tend to create positive influences or negative influences. More than likely, a social reality is more positive and enjoyable when its members contribute positive commentary. Conversely, those who add complaints or demeaning remarks likely bring down the mood of their recipients. Thus, participating in conversations that reflect Jesus will support a preferred social reality founded on Jesus.

When I was in high school, I found myself in a confusing world based on my various social realities. At home, our conversations were intellectual and challenging. At school, my conversations were immature and ungodly. At church, the conversations were godly and fun. And with God, my conversations were desperate.

Now, of all the different conversations I hear, I can choose to listen to the ones that speak truth rather than lies.

As a direct result, I lived a confusing adolescence. But neither you nor I have to live in confusion, for our God is not a God of confusion, but of peace (1 Corinthians 14:33). Now, of all the different conversations I hear, I can choose to listen to the ones that speak truth rather than lies.

By Word of Mouth

But sometimes differentiating between truth and lies is difficult in a world of mixed signals. Perhaps the best way to combat this confusion is by listening to the most important conversation over all the others. Rather than comparing ourselves with others based on appearance, social status, or economic class, we should see ourselves in light of who we are in Christ and construct our social reality based on His conversation to us through His Word. The conversations we have with others may have an influence on us, but if others' influences contradict God's construction of our reality, then we know those influences are lies.

And our social reality dwindles down to the sole fact that we are His. We belong to God—the Creator of the Universe—who knows us by name and loves us enough to save us from our sins and redeem our sins.

For all who are led by the Spirit of God are sons of God. For you did not receive the spirit of slavery to fall back into fear, but you have received the Spirit of adoption as sons, by whom we cry, "Abba! Father!" The Spirit himself bears witness with our spirit that we are children of God, and if children, then heirs—heirs of God and fellow heirs with Christ, provided we suffer with him in order that we may also be glorified with him.

Romans 8:15–17

As children of God, we are also heirs of His eternal kingdom. Romans 7:17 says that we will be glorified with Jesus. What else matters when our own Creator chooses us despite our sin to receive eternal glory with Him? Dwelling within this conversation with our God through His Word by means of the Holy Spirit is the only true social reality on which we can base our identities forever. How God sees us does not change with societal demands or ideals, but His view of us is as steadfast as He is, enduring through all the ages (Hebrews 13:8).

Determining Factor

So the use of words is important in the context of conversations. But how does language interact with reality? In other words, what kind of influence does language have on the present? If we can develop this answer, then we can formulate an even better reality.

Thinking back on that PTSD conversation, I told my roommate how I was feeling after watching the horrific car accident play across our television screen. The words I spoke determined my reality rather than explained it.[4] As I opened my mouth and processed my reality through language, I determined what I was experiencing. I did not already know how I was feeling, nor could I fully explain my experiences; as my roommate talked with me, our discourse produced a new understanding of my reality. Deciphering between whether language determines or explains realities will help create a reality that shapes rather than passively accepts reality.

The Scriptural example I gave in the previous section applies here equally as well. When Jesus told the woman she was healed, He determined that reality for her. Although Jesus is omniscient (which, therefore, could lead to an argument that Jesus merely explains reality from His perspective), He uses language to determine the reality that *we* understand. We are not omniscient and therefore need language to understand one another (as we have previously discussed). Through Jesus's language, the woman's reality changed. Had Jesus used language to *explain* her reality, He would not have been proactive about changing it but merely observing and explaining it as though He had no interference in the matter.

If we base our assumptions of language on the fact that it merely explains reality, then we are automatically stuck, not able to determine anything different from what we are explaining. When we explain, we talk about something that already happened or something that is static rather than leaving the explanation open for alternative determinations. Explanation limits; determination activates change.

For example, once someone explains his or her experience, no one can argue against that experience. However, if talking about the experience determines its meaning, then discussion with others expands beyond the individual's experience—it extends to touching others' experiences and changing them as well.

With my roommate, my internal language and my verbal language determined my reality. Had I explained my experience, my situation would have been much more discouraging, for what power would I have had to change it? However, by stating that I was feeling distress as a result of seeing the car accident imagery, I determined many things: PTSD is real; I was experiencing a symptom of PTSD; and I would need to find a way to overcome it. I did not have to stay discouraged. I could have hope. And I determined that hope by using my words.

This shift in mindset gives power to how we can understand and formulate our identities. Rather than explaining what others say about us or what society says about who we should be, we can determine who we are by proclaiming God's truth about us. Knowing that language has power to change rather than depress can only add to how we begin to change the process from seeing ourselves as worthless to seeing ourselves as having great value—enough value for Someone to die on the cross for our eternal benefit.

Reflect:

☐ What are some of your go-to phrases? If you can't think of many, you could ask your friends over social media; that's always fun.

☐ How do you abide in God's Word?

Practice:

☐ Okay, I've got a fun activity here. Pull out your smartphone and go to your best friend's message screen. If you have predictive text turned on, the predictive text options should appear above your keyboard. Type the middle option 15-ish times and see what kind of sentence pops up. And then laugh or smile because it's funny or an accurate depiction of you. Or cry hysterically because 15-ish bad words popped up. And just for fun, play with the first and third slots of the predictive text, because for some reason, my third slot always types in all caps, and that's weird because I DON'T YELL OVER TEXT.

☐ One more activity: Genuinely compliment someone this week. As much as we tear each other down with comparisons, we need some encouragement from each other. And keep complimenting. Don't stop after you've gotten your compliment in for the week. Keep going.

Chapter Six
Interchange Changes

Similar to how talking with a counselor helps some people get through difficult times, writing is therapeutic for me. I have always been a lover of journaling, taking down notes avidly, and writing book after book. Although I usually dislike my finished work and choose to start on another idea, I know that every time I pen a word, that word does not return empty. This certainty held especially true after God began working on redefining my concept of identity.

I was learning about the power of prayer, something I mentioned often yet rarely considered with much weight. But God worked through a stranger's prayer over me while I lay in a patch of grass next to our battered Jeep. I am no nurse, nor am I an expert in the medical realm, but I had a lacerated liver—a major organ—and never had to undergo surgery. The moments when the pain intensified after the shock wore off may have been the scariest moments of my life, but I was not in as much peril as I could have been. When the EMTs checked my vital signs, my life was not in danger.

I wondered if I would have been in danger had God not chosen to work through that stranger's prayers in those intense moments. That is certainly possible, but I have no way of knowing. All I do know is that God was present, holding my life in His hands through a stranger's prayer on my behalf.

A few months after the accident, I was reflecting on that moment and considering the power accessible through prayer (Proverbs 21:1, 20:24, 19:21). So I began another one of my writing projects.

This project was kind of like blogging, except I limited the audience to my eyes only. I called it "41 Days of Answered Prayer" during which I started my day writing a prayer and ended my day writing about how God worked in my life that day. Through those times, I found power in seeing God's faithfulness to provide exactly what I needed every day. This example of His faithfulness was powerful for me, for I was in the middle of rediscovering who I was in Christ rather than depending on my old ways of defining my sense of self by comparing myself to other imperfect people. And I moved forward in rediscovery by writing.

But what was perhaps even more powerful than simply writing out these prayers and making notes of answered prayers was reading them out loud.

My roommate, who is also a Christian, would graciously listen while I read my musings aloud to her. When I read aloud, the words became more real than they had been before. This idea makes perfect sense when we recognize that when we speak, we take some sort of position. Whether for or against the issue at hand, our words usually convict us more than anyone else.

In Tow

I mention the "41 Days of Answered Prayer" project because something especially powerful happened on day 10. The following is what I wrote that day:

I am not a crier, but as I sit here typing, tears keep sliding down my cheeks.

Because I am just so frustrated right now. And angry. And scared. I have not been in a place like this in a long time, and after holding it together over the last hour or so, I am finally letting myself feel the emotion of what has happened tonight.

My car got towed. And for me—the one who always follows the rules—I read the towing signs that were next to the parking lot, but the sign read that the lot was available for patrons only. No clarification as to which store, restaurant, or building I had to be a patron for was apparent, so I parked there. A few other cars were there, but the lot was mostly empty. Perhaps I should have realized that the parking lot was emptier than the others for a reason, but I assumed that the emptiness was a result of it being farther away than the other lots.

I had met with my city group [church group] for some fellowship at a rooftop restaurant, and the entire time spent with them was rich and rewarding. I was filled with joy at spending time with them.

But when I got to the parking lot and could not see my car anywhere in sight, everything changed.

And when I called the number on the sign, the lady informed me that I would have to pay $293 to get my car back.

Two hundred ninety-three dollars!

Over the last few weeks, I had already been struggling financially. Buying textbooks wiped me out, and because I was working much fewer hours at my part-time job, I had not been receiving my usual income.

This is a hard place for me right now, knowing I have less than $200 to my name.

Just typing it scares me.

I honestly do not know what to do from here. I do not understand why this had to happen to me, and I do not know why God would place this obstacle in my life today.

But I also realize that it is not up to me to know why God does the things that He does. He is sovereign and is working things together for my good (Romans 8:28). He is for sure calling me to trust Him right now, for I can in no way rely on myself. I am already feeling overwhelmed with graduate school, homework, a part-time job, and my teaching assistant job. My low income makes me feel like I need to get a weekend job, but I don't know if my stress levels can handle it.

As I go through this uncertainty, I can at least trust that God can handle it. I know Satan is persecuting me right now because I am doing everything in my power to do God's work and to show people how mighty my God is. I am disheartened, but not faithless. God will provide.

> *We are hard pressed on every side, but not crushed; perplexed, but not in despair; persecuted, but not abandoned; struck down, but not destroyed.*
> 2 Corinthians 4:8 NIV

Satan likes to attack us for doing God's work, just like he is attacking me now. Now, it's time for me to brush the tears from my eyes, ask the Holy Spirit to come down and comfort this annoyed spirit within me, and tell the devil to bring it on.

Because there is nothing he can do to stop me from praising my God—not even towing my car.

That was a tough day, but I began to feel more empowered as I wrote out what I was feeling. At first, I felt hopeless and scared, but as I kept pouring forth my heart, I knew that my heart trusted God above my wallet. Because writing allows me to voice my thoughts, often more clearly than when speaking, writing that excerpt was the first step in taking a stand against the anxiety that had begun to overwhelm my joy.

However, I did not stop there. Rather than simply leaving the content on the computer where it would be unavailable for anyone else to read or benefit from, I chose to read it out loud to my roommate. Doing so made what I had written even stronger than it had been when it was just between God and me. I was not keeping my faith to myself; I was sharing it, and by sharing it, I felt even more empowered than before.

Because I had someone else listening, I had someone holding me accountable for the actions that my words preached.

Because I had someone else listening, I had someone holding me accountable for the actions that my words preached. No longer could I sway back and forth between fear and faith because I no longer concealed my struggle. I took a stand against the fear by proclaiming my faith in God's provision.

And I have to brag on God a bit here—the next day, my stepdad deposited a substantial amount of money into my account. Because this was so rare, I knew that God worked on my stepdad's heart to lead him to give in such a way. God really does provide.

The idea that speaking takes a position proves that our words are powerful.[1] Thus, when we combine speaking with words from God's Word, would not our words be even more powerful? Better yet, what if when we spoke, we spoke words of worship rather than words of evil?

First, the Bible instructs us on what our words should sound like: "Let no corrupting talk come out of your mouths, but only such as is good for building up, as fits the occasion, that it may give grace to those who hear" (Ephesians 4:29). When we speak wholesome grace over others and over ourselves, we walk in step with God's Word and, as a result, feel the power of grace replacing fears of the unknown. When we allow ourselves to speak words that do not build up others or ourselves, we act in disobedience and, as a result, do not feel empowered by grace but rather crippled by fear. We have a choice to either take a stand against death by proclaiming life or take a stand against life by proclaiming death. No middle ground exists for our words; when we speak, we either uplift or tear down.

When our words are words of worship, we also find that we are in step with who Jesus predestines us to become: "For those whom he foreknew he also predestined to be conformed to the image of his Son, in order that he might be the firstborn among many brothers" (Romans 8:29). We are being made to look like Christ. Each day that we have breath, we draw nearer and nearer to our time to die and continue our lives with God forever. Although we will not reach perfection on earth, for no one is good (Romans 3:11), God will complete the good work that He began in us at the day of Jesus Christ (Philippians 1:6). As we continue speaking in a manner that Christ approves, we also continue looking more like Him, which is in alignment with God's work in our lives (1 John 3:1–3).

Thus, when we worship Jesus, we become more like Jesus.

To exemplify this concept, I want to introduce something that one of the pastors of my church sometimes does. Pastor Ryan Keeney sometimes "inverses" a Bible verse or passage to show the contrast of living for the world versus living for Christ. In talking about worship, he used the following passage:[2]

Psalm 135:15–18	Psalm 135:15–18 inversed
The idols of the nations are silver and gold, the work of human hands. They have mouths, but do not speak; they have eyes, but do not see; they have ears, but do not hear, nor is there any breath in their mouths. Those who make them become like them, so do all who trust in them.	Jesus of the nations is better than the choicest silver and gold, the work of God's hands. He has a mouth and speaks; He has eyes and sees; He has ears and hears; and all breath is in His mouth. Those whom He makes become like Him, so do all who trust in Him.

Inversing the passage reveals how we look when we worship anything but God versus how we look like Jesus when we worship Him. Rather than acting as an audience in receiving criticism, hate, and degradation, we can rise up and speak against the wages of sin by declaring the grace, redemption, and love of Christ.

May we use our words to take a position for Christ that worships Christ so we look more like Christ.

Where Sin Festers

In the fall of 2015, even after I learned the power of prayer, I still didn't want to change. While I was reveling in a secret sin, I didn't want to break it off. I was not living for God; I was living for myself.

And I kept it hidden for the longest time. Even when I started seeking God after the accident, I kept this one secret sin under the rug, justifying the behavior in my mind and contradicting my sinful thoughts with actions that looked a lot like righteousness. Outwardly, I was beginning to walk the straight and narrow, but inwardly, I wrestled with a sin that attacked my mind.

I am not sure if I would have even been strong enough to talk about it, but when I recognized other people in my accountability group talking about the same secret sin with which I wrestled, I started to think I could talk about it, too.

So finally, I did. After years of thinking this secret sin was not too bad of a sin and that I was abnormal for struggling in such a way, I exposed the secret sin for what it was and brought it out of the dark where it had held absolute power over me. As a secret, it grew in power each moment I chose to withhold it from others; but as a confession, it lessened in strength.

Thus, I have found that dialogue is a lot more effective than monologue when looking to make a change.[3] I obviously did not want to change because I clung to my sin more than I clung to God, but God is always greater than our sin. And He proved it with the sweet surrender I felt in releasing the secret into the care of the women in my accountability group.

Secrets are heavy burdens, especially when we have no one with whom to share them. When adding sin into those secrets, the weight becomes unbearable. It's no wonder we struggle with identity when we are so hard-set on keeping sin concealed that it continues to rail on our thoughts. We set ourselves up for failure when we do not expose sin for what it really is.

John 3:19–20 says, "And this is the judgment: the light has come into the world, and people loved the darkness rather than light because their works were evil. For everyone who does wicked things hates the light and does not come to the light, lest his works should be exposed." Just writing out that verse makes me cringe, knowing that my failure to expose my sin is equivalent to hating the light. But by the grace of God, another woman in my group mentioned her struggle with a similar sin and gave me strength to bring mine into the light as well.

But there is a fear that comes with not wanting to confess. Just as John 3:20 says, I did not want others to think poorly of me. I wanted people—even people in my own accountability group—to think I had it all together (like that is even humanly possible). Not only was I sinning by keeping my sin in the dark, but I also was sinning by loving myself more than God.

When we worry about what others think, we place ourselves on a pedestal. We want others to like us, to think we are good, and to respect us. But the thing is, no one is good, so why do we keep pretending?

Ryan Griffith said, "Confession to one another celebrates the expiation of our sin and the sanctifying work of God through the cross of Christ (1 John 1:9)."[4] Therefore, the confession of sins is not an opportunity for hate, neither for others nor ourselves. When we confess our sin, we proclaim victory over it through Jesus Christ. He already conquered sin; He is forever victorious. We may fail, but we trust in the God who will never fail. Thus, confession may be difficult because of our internal struggles between good and evil, but once we bring it out of the dark and into the light, we can celebrate because of the sweet truth that we do not have to be perfect. Jesus was perfect for us and gave us the Holy Spirit to help us in our times of need. He is making us more like Him, and this refinement grows in confession and repentance of sin.

Any possibility of changing from a life controlled by sin to a life led by Christ starts with decreasing the power of sin by proclaiming God's grace over confession to God and others. Once I shared my sin, I brought it to light and lessened darkness's hold over my heart. We can continue decreasing the power of sin by constantly declaring the truth of the gospel over our sin in confessions to our brothers and sisters. We do not have to struggle alone, nor are we supposed to. We have a body of believers for many reasons, and we are to "bear one another's burdens, and so fulfill the law of Christ" (Galatians 6:2). We fulfill the law of Christ by caring for one another, which means caring about others' sins and carrying those burdens with grace.

Together, we can use our dialogue to increase atmospheres of light and decrease the darkness the monologue of sin could otherwise maintain.

Engaging with Change

As I spoke my sin into the open, it lost power. Before I chose to confess it, though, something else also started to happen.

When other women in my accountability group started talking about their specific sins, my heartbeat immediately quickened. This was supposed to be a pleasant lunch with girlfriends, but I was anxious talking about sin as if it had no hold on them. I wondered how they could talk like that—as if it were okay to talk about our struggles. But they kept graciously talking about their issues, and even if we did not all wrestle with the same shortcomings, I knew I had to digress from the surface-level sins I had previously shared. I knew I had to get to the nitty-gritty of my heart problem.

As we exchanged information in that conversation, change already began to happen. That was obvious with my physical responses to their comments.[5] Before I confessed my own sin, simply hearing others share their sins changed my attitude toward my own. Rather than wanting to hide the sin, I began to want to be rid of it. And this all started happening simply with the interchange of information between them and me.

This kind of revelation proves that we do not have to share information to begin to change. Change automatically happens whenever someone else shares something from his or her own heart. Whether that change leads to action or awareness, the change is still occurring. When this change begins to happen, the sin shrinks back into its own darkness and away from our light.

Change begins simply through interacting with others, but change becomes even more productive when we take action upon what God places on our hearts. The beauty of trusting our change with God is that He never changes (Hebrews 13:8). Change is inevitable on our end, whether to our detriment or to our benefit. But no matter what changes come our way, we can trust in the unchanging, holy God to use our change for good. Therefore, we can trust that "every good gift and every perfect gift is from above, coming down from the Father of lights, with whom there is no variation or shadow due to change" (James 1:17). Even in trials and difficult change, we know that the end result will always be for our good and God's glory (Romans 8:28) because He does not change. He will always be good, even when we are not.

So as we work toward decreasing sin and increasing Jesus in our lives (John 3:30), we know that in the end, darkness will vanish: "The night is far gone; the day is at hand. So then let us cast off the works of darkness and put on the armor of light" (Romans 13:12). Many have heard of the biblical example of the armor of God in Ephesians 6—this is the armor of light. As we continue to put on the armor of light and bring to light the deeds we have kept in the dark, the darkness will retreat. God will have victory, and I want to fight on the winning side.

When we decrease darkness, our lives begin to look more like light. Not only do our lives change as a result of retracting sin from our hearts, but we also change. As we seek a solid identity that can only be found in Christ, we lean on the unchanging One for support. If we begin to place our identity on how we change rather than placing our identity in the One who allows us to change, then we will again fall privy to sin in a different nature.

As we reduce the sin in our hearts, we automatically look more like the Light of the world. However, God alone deserves praise for any positive change in us. Since there is nothing good in us (Romans 3:10), we cannot change without God's good power working in us. We can bring about an identity that looks more like Christ through interacting with others, bringing about positive changes, and trusting in God's power alone to do so.

Reflect:

- ☐ Who will listen to your darkest sins without judgment?
- ☐ What secret sin disrupts your obedience to God?

Practice:

- ☐ Confess your secret sin to someone who can handle it without judging you. If you don't have someone, start your own accountability group. All you need is a couple of women. Trust that your vulnerability will tie you together, so confess. Know that confession is the beginning of breaking free from the entanglement of sin. I beg you not to ignore this one. Find someone or a few someones to hold you accountable; they likely need accountability, too. We need each other to push back darkness, and we do this by being a community of light and judgment-free confession.

Chapter Seven
Community Communicates Christ

In those moments of uncertainty immediately after the accident, I relied on others to take care of me. In an individualistic culture, we often rely on ourselves, independent of others, to function. And just as the accident would not have progressed the same way had I been alone, nothing in life happens inside a vacuum. I would have found safety much more slowly had I been the only survivor with no one else there to make an emergency call. I would not have been rescued by those people in blue hospital suits if they had never learned from others how to care for people in the midst of emergencies. Nor would I have been in the wreck in the first place had I lived my life in isolation, which is also impossible when surrounded by a world of other people. In all, I would not have been on that Florida vacation if I had been the sole creator of my reality. People influence other people's lives regardless of whether people desire that influence or not. My family has influenced me beyond just our July family vacation, and other people outside my family have also impacted me in ways I may or may not recognize. Most of the time, we rely on and allow others to shape us without even realizing it.

Perhaps this point sounds simplistic, but the fact that others are equally part of creating our realities is a profound step in understanding our identities.

Created

In the beginning, God made the earth (Genesis 1:1), and He also made the first man in His image (Genesis 1:26). In other words, God created the first man (Adam) to reflect God's own image, on a much smaller scale, of course. Although many scientists put forth theories of evolution and the Big Bang, I will not discuss their theories in detail here. (The resources in Appendix A and my notes should provide sufficient explanation to begin further research on the subjects, if desired.) I will discuss, however, what is in our trustworthy account (the Bible). When Genesis 2 goes into detail about the creation of man, we also find this: "Then the Lord God said, 'It is not good that the man should be alone; I will make him a helper fit for him'" (Genesis 2: 18). God thus created a woman (Eve) as a companion for Adam. Even in the beginning of all things known to us, God knew that if He made us in His image, we would be social beings like Him, both acting as co-creators of reality. God created this social reality between humans even before sin entered the world at the Fall (Genesis 3). Co-creating reality began upon God's creation of the first people, before sin ruined the perfect community between Adam and Eve.

Similar to how reality is both mutually participative and mutually created,[1] Adam and Eve were both part of a reality they each contributed to and created. Adam could not create his reality because God had already done that by creating him. However, once God added Eve to the mix, she and Adam could both create, simply by participating with each other. Adam would speak to his wife, and she would respond, creating a conversation together. This conversation also led to new realities for both—realities that would not have come to fruition had they been alone.

We co-create with others. We cannot construct a reality alone. We do not live in bubbles of isolation in which we do nothing. We live in concert with others, walking alongside friends, family members, acquaintances, and strangers. Regardless of the level of intimacy we share with particular people, they still are part of the creative process. I cannot participate in my reality without others also participating in it. Likewise, others' lives would be incomplete without my role in their realities. Regardless of the intensity and quality, our mutual participation is the essence of our realities.

Similarly, identity is not something we form alone. I would not have found my sense of purpose had no one shared the gospel with me. I would not have known that I could live more fully had no one shown me how to live. Ultimately, I would not have known Jesus without Him revealing His grace to me through His saving work on the cross. We all participate in a reality with each other, learning more about who we are by watching how others are. But with Jesus, we can look to Him and see who He is. In learning more about Him, we find the best example of how to develop our identity. This process starts at creation.

Creator

In simply reading the first chapter of the Bible, one could argue that Adam and Eve's first conversation was not the first example of how we co-create reality. Perhaps Adam and Eve's example of participative reality was the first human example, but since God created us in His image, we know that He, too, must have a similar kind of function.

> *Then God said, "Let us make man in our image, after our likeness. And let them have dominion over the fish of the sea and over the birds of the heavens and over the livestock and over all the earth and over every creeping thing that creeps on the earth."*
>
> Genesis 1:26

As indicated in the above Bible verse, before the first human walked the earth, God was not alone (which we see through His use of the pronoun *our*). He communicated with the other Persons within His being—Jesus and the Holy Spirit. God was not isolated before time; He was completely content with and within Himself before He even created us. God was and still is and will always be God, Jesus, and the Holy Spirit—three Persons all equally and wholly God. Our finite minds may not have the capability of comprehending what may seem impossible (a being that is both completely three and completely one), but I am not sure our limited humanity could fully understand the Creator of the infinite.

However, we can understand from His being the reason behind some aspects of our own human nature, since we were, in fact, created in His image and likeness. Jonathan Edwards, in "An Unpublished Essay on the Trinity," wrote:

> And this I suppose to be that blessed Trinity that we read of in the Holy Scriptures. The Father is the Deity subsisting in the prime, un-originated and most absolute manner, or the Deity in its direct existence. The Son is the Deity generated by God's understanding, or having an idea of Himself and subsisting in that idea. The Holy Ghost is the Deity subsisting in act, or the Divine essence flowing out and breathed forth in God's Infinite love to and delight in Himself. And I believe the whole Divine essence does truly and distinctly subsist both in the Divine idea and Divine love, and that each of them are properly distinct Persons.[2]

Edwards offers a glimpse into some of the functions of God. Maybe we do not have a Father, Son, and Holy Ghost nature, but we do have a social nature that leaves us far from alone. We need our own parents for us to come into existence—our first example of an innate need for others to create our realities. As young and helpless babies, we are unable to care for ourselves and must rely on others to take care of us. As we grow into children and then adults, we still need to subsist in a world surrounded by others.

Just as I needed others to get to me where I am today,

whether by my family's Jeep crashing or someone saving my life on the side of a Florida highway, we all need others to shape us into the people we are.

Community

The Texas sun shone down on our complex's only pool, the clouds out of sight and the temperature soaring. It was more than 100 degrees now, but no one was watching their phones anymore to know for sure. Everyone was in the water. Some guys were throwing a Frisbee, and I joined in, too.

These guys were my friends; they were relaxed, liked hanging out with me at the pool, and had a welcoming posture for the gal who was new to their city. I had no other friends in my new town, so I relished the attention. Usually, I was the read-an-interesting-book-by-the-pool-and-don't-make-eye-contact-with-anyone kind of girl; but this summer, I branched out of my introverted shell. I took a stand against my shy nature and made friends. I was determined to be cool.

Okay, so maybe my roommate was an extrovert and forced me to put down my book and get in the pool with her, but still, I tried.

As a result, I surrounded myself with the people at the pool; these people were all young, fun, and up for a good time. Whether it was throwing a Frisbee for hours or eating slices of vodka-infused Jell-O in a watermelon rind, the pool was always the place to be.

After the pool, the fun usually transferred to a local bar, where this new 21-year-old danced and continued to drink more free alcohol into the dark, morning hours.

This type of community was not the best influence on me (surprising, right?). Despite my efforts to talk about my church and my God to the people at the pool, I neglected to align my actions with my words. I was just as bad as the hypocrites of biblical times:

Then Paul said to him [Ananias], "God is going to strike you, you whitewashed wall! Are you sitting to judge me according to the law, and yet contrary to the law you order me to be struck?"

Acts 23:3

Thus, my struggle with identity involved more than just wrestling with my appearance. The battle rooted from a much deeper and much wider place than that. Despite my attempts to be fun and cool around my new "friends," I felt empty, refusing to rest in the One who thought I was fine just the way I was.

Types of Community

I may have felt insecure, but I sure came across as confident. The mismatch between inward reality and external reality stresses the importance of needing a gospel-centered community that knows you and can recognize when you are straying from a life pleasing to God. My broken reality was a direct result of my lack of biblical community.

My life in a non-gospel-centered community reflected a non-gospel-centered reality.

Reconstructed

My life in a non-gospel-centered community reflected a non-gospel-centered reality. Because the people with whom I surrounded myself did not turn me to Jesus, I did not look to Jesus when making my decisions.

I want to present two different types of people who make up different communities. Most communities have a mix of both types of people. I mention only two because the Bible only mentions two whom God will separate during His final judgment. Individuals may have different personalities, sure, but God will see only two types of people spiritually.

When the Son of Man comes in his glory, and all the angels with him, then he will sit on his glorious throne. Before him will be gathered all the nations, and he will separate people from one another as a shepherd separates the sheep from the goats. And he will place the sheep on his right, but the goats on the left.

Matthew 25:31–33

This passage goes into further detail, rewarding His sheep (Christians) with "the kingdom prepared for you from the foundation of the world" (Matthew 25:34) and sending goats (non-Christians) into "eternal fire" (Matthew 25:41). Jesus made it clear in John 14:6 that the only way to inherit eternal life is through Him, saying, "I am the way, and the truth, and the life. No one comes to the Father except through me." Because Jesus is both wholly God (John 1:1–5) and wholly man (John 1:14), He is the only One through whom we can access God. Otherwise, how could any completely sinful human interact with a completely holy God? And despite cultural perspectives that good people should inherit God's

Kingdom, the Bible is clear that no one is good (Romans 3). Therefore, we all need a Savior to redeem us from our sins or else we cannot approach an inherently holy God. In addition, when Jesus restores people, He requires nothing from people to "get in." He chooses whom He chooses because He desires to choose them, not because people decided one day to be good (Ephesians 2:8). Jesus's salvation and redemption, which is the only way people can encounter God, is a gift for which we can rejoice and in which we can rest. We do not have to worry about proving ourselves worthy, because we are not worthy and never will be. But God "being rich in mercy, because of the great love with which he loved us, even when we were dead in our trespasses, made us alive together with Christ—by grace you have been saved" (Ephesians 2:4–5).

According to Scripture, then, we share our community with two types of people: Christians and non-Christians. Both are important in living the Christian life, but a healthy balance of the groups is also essential. If we are to have functioning realities, we must have properly distributed balances of different types of communities.

But what does the Bible say about what this balance between communities should look like?

Of course, the balance will look different for different Christians because each Christian has a different background, context, and set of skills.

And God has appointed in the church first apostles, second prophets, third teachers, then miracles, then gifts of healing, helping, administrating, and various kinds of tongues. Are all apostles? Are all prophets? Are all teachers? Do all work miracles? Do all possess gifts of healing? Do all speak with tongues? Do all interpret? But earnestly desire the higher gifts.

1 Corinthians 12:28

In this passage, we see that different members of the Body of Christ (otherwise known as the Church, or all Christians, not to be mistaken with just any church) have different functions within the Church. For example, teachers may spend more time exhorting than those who have more administrative gifts. Teachers may spend a different proportion of time with Christians and non-Christians than the one who spends time using his or her gifts toward more behind-the-scenes work. But all work is important in fostering the types of communities in our circles.

When we look at Jesus, we see two relational aspects of Him. He lived in contact with both His disciples and with sinners. We can both pray with and depend on other believers in gospel-centered communities so we can live the light of the Lord out to non-Christians. Having these types of groups as prevalent aspects of our lives will result in realities much more Christ-focused. A life focused on Christ is beneficial for many reasons, but perhaps one of the most important is that a life lived for Christ is a mark of a Christian. If we claim to be Christians, then we automatically strive to live as Christ did. Although we will fail, we seek to please Him out of gratitude and obedience (1 John 5:3). Therefore, when shaping our community, we can imitate the way He spent His time with people by choosing to balance our own time in a similar fashion.

Growing up in a Christian environment, I have heard many Christians talk about attending church as optional because their relationships with God are private and do not include anyone other than themselves and God. Unfortunately, many Christians have felt burned by the church or, more particularly, by the people of the church. These excuses are contrary to what the Bible teaches. Although Jesus often prayed to God alone (Luke 5:16), He spent much of His time with people—both people who followed Him and people who did not. He did not live in seclusion from His disciples; He lived in community with them. He loved those whom others condemned and welcomed them with warmth. Jesus had 12 disciples whom He turned to, drawing them from their mundane lives to follow Him, bestowing upon them a greater glory in His presence. He did not live independent of Himself. Shall we, then, not also participate in turning our friends to Jesus?

I want to encourage those who have felt hurt by church people to recognize the failure of us all (Romans 3). Christians are held to higher standards because we honor God by following His Word and example through Jesus, but we will still fall short this side of heaven. When we surround ourselves with a strong baseline of fellow brothers and sisters in Christ, we automatically have accountability for our own actions and for theirs. When we do not have a Christian community, we end up looking to non-Christians for accountability—people who live by different standards. When we have a Christian community, however, we find encouragement and grace. If other Christians do not perform up to biblical standards, then *we* have an obligation to offer grace to *them*. Anytime we offer grace to someone, we exemplify Jesus's grace to us. So regardless of how other Christians act, we can offer grace to them. When we do not have fellow Christians surrounding us, we lose that opportunity.

Jesus showed us a more excellent way by loving those who needed love the most.

Furthermore, Jesus did not just preach to those who already believed Him; He urged the disciples to spread His love to those whom the world had discarded. He ate and shared life with sinners rather than spending all His time with His church crew. He even said that it is not the healthy who need a doctor, but the sick (Mark 2:17, Luke 5:31, Matthew 9:12). He exemplified this by breaking bread with adulterers, tax collectors, and all kinds of people with whom the "holy" people of the day would not concern themselves. Jesus showed us a more excellent way by loving those who needed love the most. And He even told Peter three times after His resurrection that if Peter loved Him, he would "feed my sheep" (John 21:17). We show our love for Jesus by loving others, both Christian and non-Christian alike. We do not exclude one as though we live in a dualistic bubble.

To refuse forgiveness and reconciliation is to refuse God.

No one will be the perfect image of God, but as Jesus offers continual grace to us, we can reflect that same grace by not making generalizations about all churches based on a poor experience at one. Bashing the church offends Christ's Bride—the Church—and thus Christ. Hebrews 10:25 instructs us not to neglect to meet as Christians; so although church people will fail, God calls us to continue gathering as the people of God. To refuse forgiveness and reconciliation is to refuse God.

Furthermore, the Body of Christ shows us how the Church functions. Because each person has a different role and a different gift unique to that person, when that member of the Church is absent, the rest of the Body feels the impact.

For just as the body is one and has many members, and all the members of the body, though many, are one body, so it is with Christ. For in one Spirit we were all baptized into one body— Jews or Greeks, slaves or free—and all were made to drink of one Spirit. For the body does not consist of one member but of many. If the foot should say, "Because I am not a hand, I do not belong to the body," that would not make it any less a part of the body. And if the ear should say, "Because I am not an eye, I do not belong to the body," that would not make it any less a part of the body. If the whole body were an eye, where would be the sense of hearing? If the whole body were an ear,

where would be the sense of smell? But as it is, <u>God arranged</u>
<u>the members in the body, each one of them, as he chose. If all</u>
<u>were a single member, where would the body be</u>? As it is, there
are many parts, yet one body. The eye cannot say to the hand,
"I have no need of you," nor again the head to the feet, "I
have no need of you." On the contrary, the parts of the body
that seem to be weaker are indispensable, and on those parts
of the body that we think less honorable we bestow the greater
honor, and our unpresentable parts are treated with greater
modesty, which our more presentable parts do not require.
But God has so composed the body, giving greater honor to the
part that lacked it, that there may be no division in the body,
but that the members may have the same care for one another.
If one member suffers, all suffer together; if one member is
honored, all rejoice together. <u>Now you are the body of Christ</u>
<u>and individually members of it</u>.

1 Corinthians 12:12–27; emphasis added

This passage is essential in understanding the Bible's view
on community. The Body of Christ (our reality as Christians)
does not consist of one individual; the Body consists of many
parts (Christians), who all have something to offer. If one
member is not present, then the rest of the Body knows and
expresses concern. In a similar manner, this is how a Christian
community should function: turning members to Jesus.

Perhaps some of the most gospel-centered communities
have a mix of Christians and non-Christians. What better
way to witness to a non-Christian the beauty of the gospel
than by bringing him or her into the safety of a Christian

community—free of judgment. Jesus brought us into His fold, washing us free of all judgment. How much more can we bring non-Christians into our Christian fold? Gospel-centered community is powerful in uplifting its Christian members, but it is also an avenue in which Christians can share the power of the gospel with non-Christians. Simply because there are two different types of communities that God will separate on the Last Day does not mean the two are exclusive while we still reside on earth. If God has to separate people, that means they first intermingle with one another. We may not know whom God will call to recognize the power of the gospel, but we can trust that God wants to use us as His workmanship within His sovereign will.

For we are his [God's] workmanship, created in Christ Jesus for good works, which God prepared beforehand, that we should walk in them.

Ephesians 2:10

Thus, our reality with our Christian community is of high importance, for it will point us to Jesus and remind us of the sweet sayings of Scripture. However, we must not forget the point behind the Christian community, which is to make disciples (Matthew 28:19). We will not be able to make more disciples if people do not know Jesus's love (Romans 10:14); therefore, our community and our reality should include Christians and non-Christians for the ultimate purpose of loving sinners as Christ loves us.

Individual Community

The night of the accident, I could hear my mom's hysterics, my sister's crying, and my stepdad's voice. But of all the voices I heard, the one I heard the loudest was that of a complete stranger.

He had witnessed the accident and pulled over to see if we were okay. Instead of walking away, he asked if he could pray for me.

And pray he did. He prayed healing over me, and I listened, focusing on his words while we all waited for an ambulance to arrive. His automatic response to tragedy was to go out of his way and pray for complete strangers.

I hardly remember the tone of his voice; I never saw his face. But I do remember the intentional concern and his proactive steps to pray despite the traumatic scene, and I will never forget the Lord's mighty way of working through that stranger's prayers. I survived a lacerated liver, broken ribs and facial bones, bruised lungs, a damaged kidney, and the loss of eyelashes. I did not need surgery, and I have no lasting injuries. God worked through that man's prayer, and He can surely work through yours.

While community with other people is essential, we cannot neglect to have community with God. Even Jesus, while He was fully human on earth, often withdrew to pray (Luke 5:16), showing His absolute dependence on Someone other than Himself, and we should imitate Him. Through prayer, we verbalize our dependence on God and share with Him our struggles. And through prayer, God can choose to answer our prayers and work miracles.

Because we can pray to Jesus, who is petitioning on our behalf daily (Romans 8:34; Hebrews 7:25), we can talk with the God of the universe. Apart from Jesus, we would have had to make sacrifices to atone for sins (God is ultimately holy, and unholy sinners cannot approach a holy God). However, Jesus made the ultimate sacrifice for our sins so we can approach the throne of God. So why do we hesitate to take advantage of such a glorious opportunity?

Some people may argue that God works regardless of how we pray. This fact is certainly true (Psalms 107:28–30), but what if God chooses to work *through* our prayer? Why would we neglect asking for God's help when He is the only One who can help? If He is a sovereign and omnipotent God, then He is our best source of help, inside and outside our times of need.

Community includes others, but it most certainly must include God. Prayer should cross over and cover all friendships and relationships, for if we are turning to God for guidance, the Holy Spirit will grant us peace or conviction for our decisions within our communities. First Thessalonians 5:13 tells us to pray without ceasing; the best way to exemplify total dependence on God is to bring prayers and petitions to Him, just like Jesus did on earth and still continually does for us.

On the other hand, praying legalistically—as if you have to prove yourself to God—is not my encouragement. Prayer is not a checklist. Prayer is direct contact with the Spirit of God, through Jesus, to the God of the universe. When that idea gets antiquated, it is a sign to check your heart and your love for God. Do you love communicating with God? Do you love that His Word is available to you?

If not, you're not alone. But don't stay there. In Jesus, there is fullness of joy (Psalm 16:11), not half-joy or a little joy—full joy. Kevin DeYoung, in his book *Taking God at His Word*, wrote, "Our desire, delight, and dependence on the words of Scripture do not grow inversely to our desire, delight, and dependence on Jesus Christ. The two must always rise together."[3]

Dear Christian and non-Christian, Jesus's love is beckoning. His Word is enlightening, and His presence is amazing. If you're struggling in prayer, DeYoung recommends turning to God's Word. I have also heard many pastoral recommendations to read the Psalms. Regardless of where you are, you can change where you're going by reading God's Word and praying, for community with God is the root of any type of community or reality. And without communing with God, reality will be much less gospel-centered and much more self-centered. But I hope God reveals to you the glory that resides within a reality shaped by the community that comes from spending time with the most glorious God, whether that be in gospel-centered community groups, in God's Word, or through prayer.

Reflect:
- ☐ Who do you know who is not a Christian?
- ☐ Who do you call your Christian community?

Practice:
- ☐ God has created us as social beings, so get out there and make some friends—Christians and non-

Christians. If you're in a church and a small group, that is awesome; stay consistent with meeting, and confide in your friends. If you're not in a church or small group, I cannot stress enough how important community is. I know that alone time is nice; I am not saying to give up all your alone time, because I know it's precious. But we do not live in vacuums; we have people around us who have likely been through difficult circumstances, however different from our own. Our common strand of Christ breaks down social barriers and brings us together to live out godly lives. Get connected, stay connected, and enjoy the God-honoring friendships God wants to give you.

Chapter Eight
A Knack for Knowledge

Regardless of my understanding of the Bible and my immersion in Christian culture, I have still fallen short and placed my hope in feeble idols. I have already addressed a common struggle among women to look and act a certain way, but another one of my struggles relates to both genders.

As I mentioned before, about three months after the accident, the symptoms of PTSD hit. Feeling weary and bearing an uncontrollable sadness, I had no desire to go to class, yet I forced myself to attend because it is not feasible to get an "A" in graduate school with even the slightest slip in attendance. I trudged around campus with heavy eyes and no interest to participate in activities that had previously been fun. I even saw the campus counselor, who confirmed that I did, in fact, struggle with PTSD.

However, after a tearful 10-minute meeting, I found a new sense of inner strength. I went home and journaled, prayed, and wrote down specific things I could do to combat the conflict in my mind.

Knowledge Conduit

From a young age, I have always wanted to be seen as older and more mature. As the eldest sibling, I acknowledged responsibility and attempted to act as an adult should behave. Once I progressed into my teenage years, I got a job and sought conversation that would stimulate intellectual thought. I wanted to impress the adults who came for dinner with my family, and living with a lawyer as a stepdad always challenged me in a fun, lighthearted way to think of something witty before I spoke.

Before I hit the legal drinking age, I reveled in the way people expected me to be old enough to drink with them. Every time someone automatically assumed I was older than I was, I felt elated at the thought that I was one of them, yet downcast that I was not quite there yet.

But I was always one of those girls who people said acted more mature than her age. People always expected me to be older than I was, and that was a source of pride for me. I did not want to be seen as immature or too young to achieve my dreams immediately. I wanted people to take me seriously, regardless of my age. When I graduated from college a year early and made impressive grades in graduate school, I finally hoped to earn the respect that I had always wanted.

Many of you may share these sorts of experiences. However, my experiences with this self-elevating attitude only led me away from glorifying God.

I am also a perfectionist. Although I can't perfect other people and don't attempt to (at least, I don't think I do), I have always strived to perfect myself. Any Christian reading this should know that this concept as impossible, for perfection is impossible this side of heaven. As sinful beings in a sinful world, sin infects and affects everything.[1] Therefore, any hope in our own perfection will fail us.

At this point, I want to encourage you not to despair if sin is seeking to permeate your life. Even after I realized the error of my sinful ways, I still found myself bombarded by sin and falling prey to it. Much of the sin that corrupted this period of my life sprouted from a sense of pride. I took pride in how much knowledge I would acquire. I had learned throughout my childhood and adolescence that knowledge equals power. And if I could gain much knowledge, maybe then I could have the power of others' approval.

At first, knowledge may be powerful, but knowledge does not equal power because what is knowledge if one does nothing with it or does not communicate it to another? Power instead resides within the process of communicating through language, for language automatically shifts reality once we communicate with another. Furthermore, we can't obtain knowledge unless we have a language to hear, comprehend, and understand.

For example, I developed a hypothesis of my symptoms resulting from PTSD, but I had no way to confirm it until someone who was knowledgeable in the field declared it to be true. My roommate and I looked up the symptoms online and discussed the possibility, but I had no way of combating the troublesome anxiety without obtaining knowledge from someone other than myself.

Because I was not yet a licensed professional, nor was I

capable of making a minimally subjective diagnosis, I needed to communicate with someone who had the knowledge to relay information about the disorder to me before I could proceed in the healing process. I researched PTSD on the Internet until I met with the campus counselor. The knowledge I accumulated from the Internet acted as a form of communication, even if I did not interact with an individual directly, for the information on those websites came from online people to me. The Internet would not be there for us to view without someone imparting knowledge into the system through some type of language. Therefore, even if I stopped my search there, I would still have been able to affirm that knowledge only comes from communication through language, whether written text, computer code, or a human speaker.

However, I began feeling even better after meeting with the counselor than I did reading information online, for she imparted information to me that had been helpful to others—information I would not have found on the Internet. She also provided a boost of courage for me to come up with some of my own solutions. Although our time together mostly consisted of my retelling the event, it also included the counselor's guidance. I could then process that guidance into what could benefit my situation.

In the same way, any knowledge we receive only comes from God. Only the One who is omniscient, having complete knowledge of everything, could lavish knowledge upon His creation. We certainly learn from each other, but any knowledge that we share only comes from God.

A Knack for Knowledge

For I want you to know how great a struggle I have for you and for those at Laodicea and for all who have not seen me face to face, that their hearts may be encouraged, being knit together in love, to reach all the riches of full assurance of understanding and the knowledge of God's mystery, which is <u>Christ, in whom are hidden all the treasures of wisdom and knowledge</u>.

Colossians 2:1–3; emphasis added

Without Christ, we would be so entrenched in our sin that we would not comprehend the knowledge of God if it stood right in front of us (Romans 8:7), but God has graced us with Jesus, who has freed us from the enslavement of sin (Romans 6:14). Therefore, we can have knowledge of good and evil, right from wrong.

God imparts both knowledge and providence upon His creation. He communicates to us through Jesus and through His Word to reveal what we need to know to walk our faith journeys. He uses language to impart knowledge to us; we don't automatically comprehend knowledge unless Someone makes it possible to be known.

My struggle during those three months after the accident may have been with PTSD, but it was also reminiscent of my lifelong battle to achieve a certain level of intelligence or achievement. However, if knowledge only comes from God, then there is no thought or idea that I can even claim to be my own. Therefore, all knowledge that I put forth has no hold on my identity. I can desire to be the wisest of all my friends or the smartest of all my peers, but that knowledge would be in vain. As Copan observed, nothing comes from nothing.[2]

Someone has to have knowledge before he or she can pass that knowledge on to someone else, and only the One who holds all knowledge can pass a portion of it on to one who has none. This process began with the first human and has accumulated over the years so that knowledge is now abundant. But we must not forget where all knowledge comes from: God.

So I will continue to learn and offer my best in my studies so I can be the best vessel possible in bringing God glory during my time on earth, but I will not forget the words of Solomon, the king to whom God granted wisdom:

> *I said in my heart, "I have acquired great wisdom, surpassing all who were over Jerusalem before me, and my heart has had great experience of wisdom and knowledge." And I applied my heart to know wisdom and to know madness and folly. I perceived that this also is but a striving after wind. <u>For in much wisdom is much vexation, and he who increases knowledge increases sorrow</u>.*

Ecclesiastes 1:16–18; emphasis added

Reflecting on these verses reminds me to strive not for an abundance of knowledge, which is fleeting, but to contribute what I have learned to others, if the Lord sees it beneficial. Rather than striving for the things that will pass away, I can strive to love God with all my heart and serve Him with a joyful spirit, for this is the sort of knowledge that is eternal and found within the pages of the life-giving book: the Bible.

Furthermore, the act of knowing progresses from the

social realm to the individual.[3] If we are to accumulate knowledge through socializing, then we cannot have knowledge without some sort of social setting in which that knowledge can be birthed. We do not have individual knowledge without first having communication with someone with whom we can develop that knowledge—just as a child is not born with knowledge. Those who surround him or her will affect what the child knows and learns.

In community and in the Body of Christ, we automatically influence and share knowledge with each other without even trying. Simply being with others shapes what we know. We will influence other people whether we like it or not; our only power is choosing whether to be good influences or bad influences.

If we allow ourselves to participate in conversations that do not glorify God, then what we know is skewed from what is holy.

If we strive to maintain a God-honoring identity, then we should examine our social settings to know what kind of knowledge each one is imparting upon our malleable grasps of reality. If we allow ourselves to participate in conversations that do not glorify God, then what we know is skewed from what is holy. We should choose to participate in social situations that surround God. We can choose to not participate in ungodly behavior because we are freed from the slavery of sin. We have the power to choose good because we have the best on our side.

When people say that knowledge is power, I wonder if they have seen how the word *power* is used in Scripture. Every instance of the word *power* is connected to God's power, not man's. Rather than striving toward fleeting powers of the flesh, we should strive to rest in the saving love and grace of the Most Powerful, who bestows knowledge upon us as He sees fit.

Striving for knowledge can become a slippery slope into idolatry if we don't constantly examine our hearts. We must not desire knowledge over grace.

By the grace of God, we can use the knowledge He's given us to be wise with our choices in developing our sense of self. We can choose to take care of the knowledge we have, knowing to give glory to God rather than to self. This wisdom is humbling and Christ-orienting. Striving for knowledge can become a slippery slope into idolatry if we don't constantly examine our hearts. We must not desire knowledge over grace. Sure, the desire to know more reveals our unquenchable thirst for understanding—a sign that we naturally desire Something inexhaustible—but the outcome of acquiring knowledge is vanity if our source of security lies within wisdom. Instead, finding security and identity in the restful acceptance of Jesus is much sweeter and less demanding. He is the only One who can quench the thirst for knowledge because He possesses the totality of knowledge. So when we rest in His presence, we can trust that His knowledge is greater than ours, as will always be the case. We do not have to live in fear or wondering, but instead, we can drop our pride and secure our eternal hope in the only One who will completely and eternally satisfy.

Knowledge is a social phenomenon[4]; therefore, we can use the knowledge of God to share (socially) with others how good He is. Not only will this sharing increase others' awareness of the gospel, but it will also act as a reminder to us of the gospel. And the gospel, not knowledge, is power. May we who desire knowledge desire the gospel more.

Reflect:

☐ What are the most valuable pieces of knowledge you have learned over the years?

☐ When in the recent past have you used your knowledge to act wisely?

☐ How does acting wisely relate to Christian identity?

Practice:

☐ Whether we love school, hate school, or don't need school to be smart, all of us need the Bible to know more about God. No textbook or self-help book will compare to the truth found in Scripture. If you do not have a Bible, get one. If you cannot afford a Bible, one can be appointed to you; tell someone at church that you need one, and see what happens.

But don't let it lay on that side table untouched for days, weeks, and months. I often read through the Bible one book at a time. Consider starting with the New Testament and reading through one book at a time, perhaps one chapter or one section per day. Regardless of how you read, start reading consistently. The Bible is the Word of Life, so fill otherwise lifeless days with our ultimate source of life.

Chapter Nine
One Church, under God, Individual

Even in the hospital, I was making jokes. They may not have been good or funny jokes, but I still offered up positive remarks despite the pain and frustration of my situation. Rather than crying or complaining, I tried to keep the atmosphere pleasant. Maybe I responded in such a manner as a result of shock, but I think I acted the way I did more so because of my innate character that includes the need to make corny jokes.

Upon seeing my reflection for the first time, I dramatically joked that losing my eyelashes was the worst part of the whole ordeal. Rather than proclaiming the worst physical pain I had ever felt was mounting in my left side by the minute, I tried to see a bright side. The nurses, along with my mother, grinned at my optimistic character amid the trying circumstances.

I also took every opportunity available to thank everyone with whom I came in contact, including the EMTs, the nurses, and all the doctors. As they worked quickly and carefully, I realized their dedication to people's health and well-being. For someone who never had a desire to go into the medical field, I fully acknowledged the weight of what medical professionals do on a daily basis. They certainly deserve all the respect in the world, and I made sure to let them know while I was under their selfless care.

I say all of this not to brag on myself but to showcase how different we all are. I am no expert, but I can imagine that people who have experienced a traumatic event typically respond with worry and tears. That certainly would be normal, considering the impact of life-threatening situations. The difference in reactions reflects different personalities, which arise from our unique sets of social interactions. My upbringing included a goofy and fun mom who taught me to be respectful and brave; I knew how to be strong by watching her be strong. Each person grows up in a different environment because social realities are different for different people and different families, which results in a melting pot of unique personalities.

In the first psychology class of my undergraduate studies, a professor discussed the psychological debate of nature versus nurture. The general consensus seems to be that people become who they are through a combination of genetics (nature) and environment (nurture). Although I agree that both are necessary in the process of forming an identity, I will particularly focus on the environmental or social aspect of how an individual becomes an individual.

Unique

The idea of uniqueness resonates with the fact that each person arises out of his or her social interactions,[1] for how would I know I was different from someone else if that person were not present?

If I have no social interaction, it would be difficult for me to know whether my actions were acceptable or not, good or bad, right or wrong. Postmodernity or moral relativity may claim that right and wrong exists only for each individual, but each individual must determine morality based on those around them. If we lived in isolation, we would not know right from wrong.

That is, we would not know, save for the natural sensation in our heart that tells us what is right or wrong. C. S. Lewis goes into great detail about Old Testament law and how an innate sense of right and wrong reflects the fact that we have a Creator.[2] Furthermore, this sense of right and wrong comes only from what God has given us, whether we know it or not. God builds character through the moral law and thus creates unique individuals through His interaction with His creation. Moral relativists who claim that different cultures create different contexts of morality (as opposed to a natural sense of morality, which God grants His people) neglect to acknowledge what J. P. Moreland addressed in his discussion on cultural relativism:

> Cultural relativism is not a *moral* thesis at all. It is not a statement *of* morality, but a statement *about* morality. Cultural relativism is a descriptive factual

thesis which entails no substantive moral thesis.
. . . When due consideration is given to factual
clarification, cultures exhibit a widespread agreement
in basic ethical values. . . . So while some difference
may exist after factual issues are considered, there
is still widespread agreement over basic ethical
judgments. This agreement can be used as part of an
argument for some sort of natural law, or put more
theologically, general revelation, which *can* be known
by most men and is, in fact, known by most men.[3]

Moreland continued his discussion on ethical skepticism,
noting that "some moral principles can be known with more
certainty than some scientific claims."[4] These moral principles
are examples of the sense of morality that only springs from
the Law, which God ingrained on our hearts from birth.

I know that torturing babies is wrong more surely
than I know that quarks exist. It is possible, even
likely, that future physics will do away with quarks
or radically change what they are thought to be, but
it is difficult to think of future circumstances which
could revise the rationality of the claim to know that
torturing babies is wrong.[5]

In addition to describing how individuals are shaped
by their interaction with a Creator, C. S. Lewis affirms that
individuals arise from social interactions with creation. We
do not live in isolation; therefore, we live with both an innate

sense of morality gifted to us from God and a social sense of morality granted to us by His design.

> There is no reason to suppose that self-consciousness, the recognition of *a creature by itself as a "self," can exist except in contrast with an "other,"* a something which is not the self. It is against an environment and preferably a social environment, an environment of other selves, that the awareness of Myself stands out.[6]

We would not even know ourselves as being ourselves if we had no sense of otherness that comes with interacting with others. We are unique and individual to our own selves and sets of experiences. No one person can be identical to another, for each one has a different set of interactions with other individuals, therefore creating the uniqueness of each.

God's Reflection

God created us in His image, and the fact that we are each unique sheds light on God's character. As Christians and members of the Body of Christ (also referred to as the Church or Christ's Bride), we can see how each member within the Body has a unique purpose, as I mentioned earlier regarding community.

> *For as in one body we have many members, and the members do not all have the same function, so we, though many, are one body in Christ, and individually members one of another. Having gifts that differ according to the grace given to us, let*

us use them: if prophecy, in proportion to our faith; if service, in our serving; the one who teaches, in his teaching; the one who exhorts, in his exhortation; the one who contributes, in generosity; the one who leads, with zeal; the one who does acts of mercy, with cheerfulness.

Romans 12:4–8; emphasis added

The Body of Christ would not be the same if everyone were exactly alike. We are all individuals who can see that we are unique by looking to each other. As a young Christian, I can look to an older and more mature Christian to see where I am in my own faith journey. By doing so, I address my own spiritual walk and recognize it as unique to itself. No one else can have my same faith journey, and that is a very special gift indeed, for each walk is part of the sovereignty of God.

The Church, or the gathering of God's people, is not founded on a building. The apostle Paul wrote that we are God's building (1 Corinthians 3:9) who are building up on the foundation of Jesus Christ (1 Corinthians 3:11). The Church becomes sacred when the people of God meet.[7] Jesus does not take the Church lightly, so as we seek to base our foundation on Him, we must not take the Church lightly either. We need the Church; we need each other because we are "God's fellow workers" (1 Corinthians 3:9) and do not work alone. We can become more like Christ as we interact with others who look more like Christ, and this process happens through the Church.

And [Jesus] gave the apostles, the prophets, the evangelists, the shepherds and teachers, to equip the saints for the work of ministry, for building up the body of Christ, <u>until we all attain to the unity of the faith and of the knowledge of the Son of God, to mature manhood, to the measure of the stature of the fullness of Christ,</u> so that we may no longer be children, tossed to and fro by the waves and carried about by every wind of doctrine, by human cunning, by craftiness in deceitful schemes. <u>Rather, speaking the truth in love, we are to grow up in every way into him who is the head, into Christ, from whom the whole body, joined and held together by every joint with which it is equipped, when each part is working properly, makes the body grow so that it builds itself up in love.</u>

Ephesians 4:11–16; emphasis added

I find this fascinating as it pertains to identity, for as we compare to other people, we can either have hope or lose heart. God gives us an end goal so we can work as a whole (Body of Christ) rather than as a radical individual seeking to please his or her own flesh. Although society demands certain traits from both men and women, we can rely on God's goals for us, not as people alone, but as people collectively striving toward an eternal goal.

As a young woman, I have certainly felt the pressures of society to look and act a certain way. The twenty-first century provides a lot of leniency in theory and social politeness, but it has yet to deplete the kind of thinking that causes people to struggle daily with the pain of comparison.

Many have heard Theodore Roosevelt's adage,

"Comparison is the thief of joy." For anyone wrestling with his or her identity, this statement rings loudly. As we develop, we experience external stimuli such as celebrities, magazines, social media, and our peers that influence how we think we should be. As we interact with those stimuli, our sense of self shifts. As Simon Greenleaf noted, "The object of man's worship, whatever it be, will naturally be his standard of perfection."[8] When we begin to worship what we see, we see those idols as perfect, which show us our imperfections all the more. This interaction is devastating.

> The books or the music in which we thought the beauty was located will betray us if we trust to them; it was not *in* them, it only came *through* them, and what came through them was longing. These things—the beauty, the memory of our own past— are good images of what we really desire; but if they are mistaken for the thing itself they turn into dumb idols, breaking the hearts of their worshipers.[9]

When we think about how we know we are different by interacting with the different natures of others, we may find it difficult to not compare. We do it naturally, instinctively. We realize who we are only in light of how others are. We live in a society that shows how great others' lives are at the touch of a button. The comparison happens instantaneously, but how can we use that reality to form our individuality the way God wants us to?

> *If we respond to our shortcomings with overcompensation or a need to attain perfection, we develop an idol of perfection.*

The answer lies with changing whose opinion matters more—ours, others', or God's. At various points in life, we will compare ourselves with others, seeing our faults and our successes. What matters is how we respond and whose opinion we care about. If we respond to our shortcomings with overcompensation or a need to attain perfection, we develop an idol of perfection. This perfection is unattainable and will only lead to feelings of failure and insufficiency. But the completely perfect God is inexhaustibly available to His people.

> The only method, which has been successfully employed to deliver man from idolatry, is that of presenting to the eye of his soul an object of worship perfectly holy and pure, directly opposite, in moral character, to the gods he had formerly adored. He could not transfer to his deities a better character than he himself possessed. He must for ever remain enslaved to his idols, unless a new and pure object of worship were revealed to him, with a display of superior power sufficient to overcome his former faith and present fears, to detach his

affections from grosser objects, and to fix them upon that which alone is worthy. This is precisely what God, as stated in the Holy Scriptures, has done.[10]

In a world of uncertainty and unrelenting comparison, we can be certain of God's acceptance of us regardless of our depraved hearts.

Inherent Failure

One thing that we as Christians can be certain of is this: God loves us enough to have sent His Son from the heavenly realms to earth so He could die on our behalf that we may have eternal glory with Him. In a world of uncertainty and unrelenting comparison, we can be certain of God's acceptance of us regardless of our depraved hearts.

No one is sinless (Matthew 19:17), so how else could a completely holy God (Revelation 4:8) choose to save us unless it were Him doing the choosing? If there is nothing we can do to merit God's affections for us, then we know that there is nothing for us to prove to God. If God's opinion of us is the only one that matters come Judgment Day, then why listen to anyone else? Sure, we may experience the temptation to listen to Satan's lies about our identity, but God tells us that He will always give us a means of escape from that temptation (1 Corinthians 10:13). The bottom line is that we are saved because God declares us saved. What else compares to that incomparable truth?

Because we as Christians find our hope and salvation in Jesus, we also have access to God whenever we so desire. Ephesians 2:18 says, "For through him we both have access in one Spirit to the Father." When we participate in social interactions and find ourselves emerging as a new individual because of the conversation, we can check in with God to see if our comparison is godly or ungodly.

To determine whether our unique and individual self is more in tune with God's wishes for us or our own lustful desires, we have only to look at our level of contentedness.

Keep your life free from love of money, and <u>be content with what you have</u>, for he has said, "<u>I will never leave you nor forsake you</u>."

Hebrews 13:5; emphasis added
(see also Joshua 1:5)

Although Hebrews 13:5 talks about the love of money, we can apply the concept to the idolatry among Christians today. If we find ourselves content with who we are under God's declaration of who we are, then we are likely walking a life of peace rather than idolatry. However, if we find ourselves going to extremes that displease God, then we can know that we are not lining up with pleasing God and are choosing some idol over rest and contentedness in Him.

Thus, rather than being more in tune with worldly social interactions, we have the power to socially interact with God. We can pray and read God's Word, which are only two of many ways in which we can socialize with God. If we listen more intently and interact with Him more regularly, we will automatically begin to look more like Him.

Finally, the concept of contentment points us to the Body of Christ. The Church will one day unite with Jesus in the most beautiful marriage of all time (Revelation 21:2). We can look at the Church as though it is one, much like an individual. However, just as individuals develop from social interactions, so the Church develops and grows through the social interactions of its members.

The Church's members interacting with one another can have powerful implications. If the Church does not show love within its own body, how then can it show love outside the body? The Church becomes the Church each time an interaction happens. The world looks upon those interactions and either sees Jesus or sin. Therefore, if the Church is to submit to its husband, Jesus (Ephesians 5:22), then its members should submit to each other as Christ would desire. Then the Church will arise out of its members' interactions as Christ-abiding rather than hypocritical—all for the sake of bringing glory to God's name. Our interactions must look like Christ's interactions with His bride—perfect and sacrificial.

Furthermore, as the Church's interactions within the Body reflect its nature, its interactions with non-Christians show its character. Therefore, if we act and speak out of hate to those who do not know Jesus, we will become more hateful out of that negative interaction. We do not condone or promote sin; we love as Christ loves us. When we love other sinners who fail just like we fail (or differently from how we fail), we create an atmosphere of compassion that reflects the Body of Christ rather than the world. The Church can arise out of interactions with the world as loving rather than hateful. And when the Church does that, its members and non-members see Jesus.

When we love other sinners who fail just like we fail (or differently from how we fail), we create an atmosphere of compassion that reflects the Body of Christ rather than the world.

The Church's failure to live up to biblical standards does not reflect any failure of our God, because God cannot fail. Greenleaf makes an analogy of the relationship of Christians with God when he explains Christians as the rusty containers that hold the purest of all water. Although the water is pure, the containers will rust and distort the image of the goodness of the water inside.

Greenleaf urges seekers not to evaluate the truth solely on believers' behavior.

The earnest seeker must look beyond the behavior of flawed humans in order to find the truth. Would you condemn an oak tree because its timbers had been used to build battering rams? . . . No. A real evaluation of the truth of faith depends upon looking at the clean, pure water, not at the rusty containers. God cannot be judged based on our failures.[11]

But understand the weight of this responsibility. Our identities as Christians entail being members of the Body of Christ. This responsibility is not one to take lightly, for each interaction we have with others either uplifts or detracts from the Church's name. We all are part of something greater than ourselves, and each social encounter adds to how the Church's character develops. The more the Church's members love like Christ, the more the Church will look like Christ, arising from interactions within itself and with the world as loving rather than hateful.

Reflect:

- ☐ What would your closest friends or family members say your biggest character strengths are?
- ☐ For what unique purpose(s) is God currently developing you?
- ☐ How do you keep from letting comparisons steal your joy?

Practice:

- ☐ Jot down as many answers as you can think of for the three questions above. Now read them. You've got a lot going for you, right? This week, as you look around and see other women wearing cuter clothes, having smoother hair, or excelling in their areas of expertise, remember this list. If she has bright blue eyes and blonde hair that shines and you've got brown hair and brown eyes like me, please know that beauty does not stop at one type of person or look. Beauty takes many different shapes and sizes. In a culture that celebrates uniqueness, redefine what beauty means for you this week. I'm not saying hate on our blonde sisters; see their beauty but know you're just as beautiful in God's eyes. Once you've got this new definition, write it down. It's much easier to remember it that way.

Part Three

Armor That Guards

Chapter Ten
Censoring Senses

Although I boldly proclaimed the power that we have through Jesus, I did not live empowered by the gospel during the summer of 2015. I failed to restrain sin, and as a result, I failed to place my security in Jesus alone. One of the main reasons I did not uphold an identity only found in the Lord was that I neglected to *protect* my identity.

Hackers steal people's identities daily, and as a result, bankers and credit card companies have gone to great lengths to protect their clients' financial identities. If we work to protect our credit cards and bank accounts, how much more should we work to protect something as valuable as our personal, spiritual identities?

To guard identity, we must actively protect our thoughts. Our thoughts have a direct correlation to our physical senses. That means that we also must actively guard our physical senses, which "regularly meet and greet in the brain to provide accurate impressions of the world."[1] Every sensation produces a reaction in our minds. Whether it is a positive or negative reaction, the memory of an experience remains ingrained in our minds, available for reimagining or reliving whenever we so desire.

We don't automatically experience the world; we use our senses to shape our experiences of the world. We must monitor our senses because they mediate the external into the internal.

Induction of the Fittest

During and after the accident, I used my senses to process my reality. As the Jeep skidded to a stop, my mind picked up speed. Immediately, I began to process what I had seen—the flash of red of the truck pulling out in front of us. I heard the panicked voice of our family friend and the swirl of voices as the rest of my family processed out loud what was happening. I felt my body slam first against the side of the Jeep and then against the roof. And when my sister mentioned seeing smoke, I forced my nose to search for whether or not something was burning. I could not have understood what was happening without my senses.

Our senses translate external and sensory experiences into reality. We mediate and induct what we see and experience externally into what we know and process internally, all through our senses.[2] Many of these experiences happen automatically, without much thought. However, some experiences with our senses directly relate to how our minds and thoughts function. Whenever we experience something pleasurable, we often want to experience it again. In contrast, if we experience something negative, we likely will try to avoid it in the future. C. S. Lewis said it well: "And what thoughts or passions could we begin to have without objects to think and feel about? Nay, could I even begin to have the conception of 'external' and 'other' unless I had experience of an 'external world'?"[3]

We internalize what we experience externally, and we categorize experiences of the external into three areas as we induct them into our reality: pleasurable, neutral, or unenjoyable. We may automatically avoid undesirable sensations, but how do we guard against pleasurable or neutral experiences? Further, *why* should we?

> But the fruit of the Spirit is *love, joy, peace, patience, kindness, goodness, faithfulness, gentleness, self-control;* against such things there is no law. And those who belong to Christ Jesus have crucified the flesh with its passions and desires. *If we live by the Spirit, let us also keep in step with the Spirit.*
>
> Galatians 5:22–25; emphasis added

One fruit of the Spirit (indicators of a life led by Christ) is self-control. If we seek to please God in obedience (1 John 5:3), then we will also seek to have self-control. So why would we drop our self-control to maintain our identities? In a world that constantly bombards us with images and sounds and expectations that demand us to act differently from how God instructs us to behave, we have to be smart and creative about protecting against the external. How else can we protect against the internal than to first intercede for our senses?

When we compare Christianity and postmodern worldviews, we must keep in mind that "the functionality of a worldview only has effectiveness as it has application."[4] It's impossible to apply postmodernity to real-world living because everything is relative, meaning that since no one can know what is true, experience always trumps truth. However, we can effectively apply the knowledge of Christianity to guard our senses because we can use truth to help us have better experiences that both honor truth and enhance our lives. When we live for God, we experience richer, fuller identities and lives.

Sight

One thing I have noticed about American culture is that Americans are self-absorbed. This way of thinking is in contrast to how the Church ought to function in submission to God's standards. If we have an eternal goal that is not set on the flesh, then why do we allow the flesh to rule our individual desires? We have the power of the Holy Spirit and the Christian community to stand against sin, and we must take advantage of such power in the midst of a self-seeking world. But how?

First, we can place Jesus at the center of our hearts. Rather than focusing on self, we can focus on Jesus. If we can do this continually, then we can at least be change agents as we seek to transform the Christian culture from self-centered to gospel-centered.

But this is far from easy. I am the first to say that I did not place Jesus at the center of my heart even though I grew up in a Christian environment. However, as mentioned earlier, our Christian worldview helps us know what is right and how to apply it in our lives.

Sight is the sense through which most people immediately take in their surroundings. Of course, those who are blind may take in their environment through other senses, but sight allows us to take in the sensory details that allow us to navigate our environments much easier than if we did not have sight.

Now more than ever, we have constant exposure to visual stimuli. Saul McLeod explained that the brain is like a computer. The eyes receive visual information and codes that change information into electric neural activity, feeding it back to the brain where it is stored and coded.[5] He said, "This information is [sic] can be used by other parts of the brain relating to mental activities such as memory, perception and attention. The output (i.e. behavior) might be, for example, to read what you can see on a printed page."[6] We not only have billboards and advertisements demanding our attention, but we also have handheld devices that demand our attention daily. This information doesn't just pass our cornea and disappear. We automatically store the information, sending it into different categories of our brain. Technology can certainly be a gift, but we must not abuse that gift by viewing images that can scar our memories with ungodliness. Rather than sitting back and letting the permanent scarring happen, we can put on the armor of God to defend our minds.

Finally, be strong in the Lord and in the strength of his might. Put on the whole armor of <u>God, that you may be able to stand against the schemes of the devil.</u> For we do not wrestle against the flesh and blood, but against the rulers, against the authorities, against the cosmic powers over this present darkness, against the spiritual forces of evil in the heavenly places.

Ephesians 6:10–12; emphasis added

Although we may be under siege, we are not helpless. We can stand against Satan's attacks on our identity. He may want us to think we are not pretty enough, strong enough, fit enough, or smart enough. But the simple truth that Christ died on our behalf shows that it does not matter what we are. Our lives are not about us; everything points back to Jesus. We will never be good enough (Matthew 19:17), but Jesus will always be more than good enough. That is why we can place our identity securely in Him rather than insecurely in ourselves.

Thus, whenever our eyes see things that do not point us to the Lord, we have a choice to look away or use Scripture (Ephesians 6:17) to combat sinful images that may lure us away from a Christ-centered mind. Rather than letting sin slip into our sight, we must seek the One who gives us sight so that we can see His eternal glory rather than focus on the inglorious nature of sinful imagery.

Sound

In a similar fashion, we take in external sounds and induct them into our reality just as quickly, or even more quickly, than sight. Sounds can be intentional or unintentional, but we can always be intentional about what we allow to transfer from what we hear to what we think.

For example, crudeness is more widely accepted now than ever. People find crude humor funny and disrespectful music catchy. As a result, our culture has become insensitive to offensive lyrics and words as well as to those whom they offend. What may be worse is that some people have grown indifferent. Barton Gingerich, who writes for the Gospel Coalition, said, "With the rise of the Millennial generation in evangelical churches, a vice is creeping up into the realms of acceptance, indifference, or at least resignation."[7] He continued to write specifically on the topic of sex, but his point still stands regarding Millennial tolerance. Our generation seems to be generally more accepting of sin than previous generations, especially when that sin satiates our desires. When people surround themselves with other people who speak out of hate or dishonor, both parties may end up participating in the same disrespectful content, creating an ungodly environment. "Do not be deceived: 'Bad company ruins good morals'" (1 Corinthians 15:33). As Charles P. Barnard and Bruce P. Kuehl explain of Thomas Reik's Law of Reciprocal Affect, "what people demonstrate to others is exactly that which they are most likely to receive back."[8] Thus, a slippery slope of sin becomes a more enticing and possible route for those who participate in sin freely.

However, Christians have a mandate to go into the world and love as Jesus loved us. We can and should surround ourselves with others who do not know Him, but we should also prepare for those meetings as though going into battle. We cannot expect to defeat temptation if we do not prepare for tempting encounters with the world.

> *Therefore, take up the whole armor of God, that you may be able to withstand in the evil day, and having done all, to stand firm. Stand therefore, having fastened on the belt of truth, and having put on the <u>breastplate of righteousness</u>, and, as shoes for your feet, having put on the <u>readiness given by the gospel of peace</u>. In all circumstances take up the shield of faith, with which you can extinguish all the flaming darts of the evil one; and take the <u>helmet of salvation</u>, and the <u>sword of the Spirit</u>, which is the <u>word of God</u>, <u>praying at all times in the Spirit</u>, with all prayer and supplication. To that end, <u>keep alert with all perseverance</u>, making supplication for all the saints, and also for me, that words may be given to me <u>in opening my mouth boldly to</u> proclaim the mystery of the gospel, for which <u>I am an</u> <u>ambassador</u> in chains, that I may declare it boldly, as I ought to speak.*
>
> Ephesians 6:13–20; emphasis added

In Scripture, God tells us exactly how to prepare for battle against the flesh and against temptation. He provides a way out of any temptation we encounter, and in the short passage above, He gives several specific applications:

- ☐ Rather than listening to the lies of Satan that we have to be or act a certain way because society tells us so, we can cling to the *belt of truth*, which tells us that "while we were still sinners, Christ died for us" (Romans 5:8). We all fall short, so no amount of effort will make us more acceptable in God's sight. But Jesus accepts us in spite of us, and He died to save us.

☐ Rather than participating with crude musical lyrics and humor that dishonor others and God, we can hold tight to the *breastplate of righteousness*: "For our sake he made him to be sin who knew no sin, so that in him we might become the righteousness of God" (2 Corinthians 5:21). Through Jesus alone, we are God's righteousness.

☐ Rather than being anxious about the comparison game, we can have *the readiness given by the gospel of peace* because "he himself is our peace" (Ephesians 2:14). We do not have to wallow in worry; we can be ready to stand with peace.

☐ Rather than accepting negative words and slurs, we have *the shield of faith* in the assurance of our eternal *helmet of salvation* (Hebrews 11:1), which is of far greater value than fleeting acceptance of what seems cool.

☐ Rather than depending on human judgment, we can listen to God through His infallible Word and use Scripture to attack sin with the *sword of the Spirit*, similar to how Jesus refuted temptation with *Scripture* (Matthew 4).

☐ Rather than taking in sounds or words that deflate our zeal for God, we can *pray continually* (1 Thessalonians 5:17). We can change the radio channel to hear songs that don't dishonor what God calls sacred.

- Rather than being lazy against satanic attacks, which occur through the transfer of sound to thought, we can *stay alert and stand firm* in the "true grace of God" (1 Peter 5:12).

- Finally, we can combat words and sounds and music that lead to sin and destruction of righteousness by *proclaiming the grace of God* instead. We can do this through speaking of our Lord *boldly* because of our full confidence in Him (Ephesians 3:12).

- Therefore, we have hope that although we mediate the sense of sound from external to internal, we have the power of the Spirit to filter what external sounds affect our minds. Rather than allowing sinful sounds to infect our thoughts, we can choose to deflect those thoughts with sounder, stronger minds devoted to the Word of God and mouths that replace ungodly chatter with righteous words of life.

Touch

Almost everyone wants to feel loved. Our society (in America, at least) often equates love with lust,[9] which leads us longing for more and more, never finding satiation. That is because lust is temporal. Beauty will fade, moments of passion will pass, and people will disappoint.

The media plays a large role in how much we dwell on lust. Through television, radio, and pop culture, we see people partying, participating in premarital sex, and living for nothing but the pleasure of their own flesh. The media tells us that lust is satisfying and sin is normal. It tells us that we should not only tolerate sin but celebrate it, because after all, why would God want us to be unhappy?

That mindset is what reminds us that the root desire does not come from the media, although it most certainly plays an influential role.

As I quoted earlier, "Sin infects and affects every area of our lives."[10] Ever since Eve succumbed to sin in the Garden of Eden, we have been plagued with a desire for ourselves and not for God. We love lust because we love to satisfy the flesh. We may start as singles with a good desire for future intimacy with a spouse we hope to one day meet, but sin works on our hearts to produce a desire for intimacy, period. This desire may lead to an abundance of evil practices that lead us away from the desire that God designed to be holy.

But what we or Satan may intend for evil, God intends for good (Genesis 50:20). God shows us perfect love by having His own Son lay down His life for our eternal glory (Romans 5:8), and 1 Peter 4:8 tells us that "love covers a multitude of sins." God has a perfect plan for His creation, and it includes His love covering our sins with Christ's blood. When we truly see God's loving sacrifice for us, we want to both love Him and love like Him. "Our only hope as an insatiable being is in a God who is inexhaustible."[11] Because we have a God who is inexhaustible, we have hope. Our longing hearts can only be satisfied in Him. Nothing else will satiate our otherwise unquenchable thirst.

Therefore, as we trust and rely on the One who satisfies, we can also avoid the ways of the flesh that lead to death by first guarding against sights and sounds. Then we can be wise in protecting God's temple: "Or do you not know that your body is a temple of the Holy Spirit within you, whom you have from God? You are not your own, for you were bought with a price. So glorify God in your body" (1 Corinthians 6:19–20). My body is not mine to destroy with sin; it belongs to God and God alone.

Rather than placing ourselves in situations that would jeopardize this temple, we must regard it with respect. We must stand guard and use the sense of touch for God's glory and not our own.

> *I appeal to you therefore, brothers, by the mercies of God, to present your bodies as a living sacrifice, holy and acceptable to God, which is your spiritual worship. Do not be conformed to this world, but be transformed by the renewal of your mind, that by testing you may discern what is the will of God, what is good and acceptable and perfect.*
>
> Romans 12:1–2

Taste and Smell

I ran a lot, trying to get my body in shape for the summer after my 21st birthday. I loved the heat and the opportunity to lie by a pool and tan. The not-so-fun part of it was eating a lot of greens during the day or not eating much at all.

The places where I spent weekend evenings were filled with smoke-polluted air and a constant flow of adult beverages. I never smoked, but the smoke at those places caused me to wake up the next morning with an extremely dry feeling in my chest. Sometimes I woke up a little more slowly than usual, feeling the residual effects of no longer qualifying to be the designated driver.

Just thinking back on those weekends makes me sick. I didn't know it, but I idolized myself then. I spent every day working on how I could make myself look more appealing rather than focusing on how I could showcase God in a more glorifying way.

That is why I have found that guarding the senses of taste and smell is just as important as guarding the other three senses.

Have nothing to do with irreverent, silly myths. Rather, train yourself for godliness; for while bodily training is of some value, godliness is of value in every way, as it holds promise for the present life and also for the life to come.

1 Timothy 4:7–8; emphasis added

So practicing discipline with food can be a way to show self-control, which is a fruit of the Spirit, but practicing idolization with food may be an indicator that a love for a fit body may extend beyond a love for God.

Eating healthy can also be beneficial, for 1 Corinthians 6:19–20 does tell us to honor God with our bodies. However, when we begin to idolize food as we elevate our bodies to a higher standard, we lose sight of the purpose of eating healthy. We can certainly be good stewards of our bodies and feed them well, honoring God and preparing our bodies for however He wants to use us, but we must not do so to such an extent that we care more about food than we do about God. Basically, eating healthy is a good thing, but 1 Timothy 4:8 tells us that godliness is the best thing. A cheat day will not cause God to love you any less than He already does. So practicing discipline with food can be a way to show self-control, which is a fruit of the Spirit, but practicing idolization with food may be an indicator that a love for a fit body may extend beyond a love for God.

On the opposite end, alcohol is not sinful when you drink with control. Jesus drank wine; we too can enjoy that with which He has blessed us. However, when we participate in drunkenness, we are falling into sin, taking a good thing and making it a god.

A smell is typically a good indicator of setting. For example, those places where I spent my weekends did not smell good because they were not good places to be. Therefore, if something does not smell right, perhaps we can check our location and decide whether or not it is a place where we can glorify God. Sure, some bars may be a good place to share the gospel, but most bars do not have a quiet environment where conversation can flourish. A dance club where no one can hear each other and people are dancing inappropriately, smoking, and consuming too much liquor may not be the most conducive setting for sharing the gospel.

Furthermore, "we are the aroma of Christ to God among those who are being saved and among those who are perishing" (2 Corinthians 2:15). When people encounter us, do they "smell" Christ in us?[12] If not, one way to start is by putting on the perfume of grace. We have the fragrance of life (Jesus), even if we are insufficient for it. But God graces us with it anyway, so we, in turn, want to extend that grace to others. When we do so, the aroma of Christ starts to fill rooms and replace smells of death with scents of life.

Faith

Although faith is not one of the five senses, it encompasses how we use all of them. We induct the external into internal reality through the senses, but faith is what drives our will to guard our senses in the first place.

If faith is the only thing that pleases God (Hebrews 11:6), then as believers in Jesus Christ's resurrection for our salvation, we want to please God with our faith. When we trust God rather than trust our flesh, we find much more stability. Despite the turbulence of life, we have a stronghold to Whom we hold fast. Because we have faith in God, we can trust that He gives us a way out of temptation (1 Corinthians 10:13) and the strength to persevere until the day He calls us home into perfect eternity (Philippians 1:6). When we have that kind of faith, we can cling to that kind of secure identity.

So we are always of good courage. We know that while we are at home in the body we are away from the Lord, for we walk by faith, not by sight.

2 Corinthians 5:6–7

Therefore, everything that we allow to enter our minds and take hold in our hearts should reflect a mind and life set on Christ rather than the flesh. Although it may be difficult in a world bombarded with sin, we have the power of the God of the universe to help us overcome. And if we struggle to combat the sensory experience of the external, we can not only ask for wisdom, but also receive it (James 1:5). May we ask for wisdom and apply Scripture to censor our senses as we bring our external world into our realities that are set on Christ.

Reflect:

- ☐ What are the main things that you think about?
- ☐ How do you think about these things?
- ☐ What external experiences cause these thoughts?

Practice:

- ☐ Write down one way to protect each sense so that you can thus protect your heart. Now practice these techniques this week and see how things shift.

Chapter Eleven
What's Wrong with Being Confident?

Although I will not be that girl who blames all her mistakes on "daddy problems," I am aware of the influence that my "daddy problems" had on how I understood my reality from a young age. Not meeting my biological father until I was a senior in high school resulted in questions about what it was about me that made him not want to be involved in my life. Finding a father figure in my mom's first husband only to experience rejection with the divorce made me doubt that true love was ever possible. And losing my Papa—my grandpa—the only man who had been there through all of it—to heart problems made me realize that daddies would never be permanent.

I could have let it all get to me, but I did not want to wallow in self-pity—at least I did not think I did. But during my high-hormonal high school years, a bitterness toward not only dads, but guys in general became ingrained in my heart subconsciously. Yet when guys gave me even the slightest attention, I automatically let my guard down, relishing the attention I never received from any of my dads. And when they, too, broke my heart, I learned that trust was transient and love impossible—at least for someone like me.

So, yes, I basically wallowed in self-pity, journaling hateful entries about guys, praying out loud in anguish, and learning how to bury all the emotions that came with my stressed-out teenage life. I buried them so deeply into my gut that I became absent of emotion. Nothing and no one would hurt me if I did not allow anyone to get close enough to make an impact.

I lived like this year after year, guy after guy, until I finally reached my breaking point.

I am not proud to admit it, nor am I trying to dramatize a sensitive subject. However, I know I was not the only teenager to struggle with such feelings, and I know many more have struggled since. People may try to cover it up and pretend everything is okay, but I will not be one of those people. People talk about high school struggles as if they are just a phase and not a big deal, but no high schooler feels the depths of his or her raging emotions and considers them to be just a phase. We have to take young people seriously or else they will feel just as alone as I felt and act to the extremes that I acted.

My emotions were high, yes, but my mind still raced with existential questions. During those high school years, I let myself replace feelings of helplessness with feelings of physical pain as I practiced self-harm. I was lost and felt as if that was the only direction I could turn. With problems in our household, I also distanced myself from family members. I felt utterly alone.

But God rescued me from those dark places and gave me a reason to live differently. Those moments of despair were the accumulation of my past experiences, which had altered the way I perceived my reality. I took the negative aspects of my family history and automatically used them to make judgments on the rest of the world, resulting in my falling prey to negative thinking and pessimistic living.

Making Sense of Nonsense

Our brains automatically structure our experiences in a way that makes sense and catalogue our experiences based on familiar past experiences.[1] Rather than trying to formulate reality based on what does not make sense, we organize reality based on the logic of our own sensations and perceptions.

I organized my negative reality based on my negative experiences with guys. They hurt my feelings, so I began to assume that all guys would hurt my feelings. So I grew callous toward men because it made sense for me to protect myself in such a way. And when I began experiencing problems within my own family, I grew distant from them as well. Therefore, I processed my experiences in a manner that made me consider the loner life as the best life.

Now I know that my family experiences are nowhere near as dramatic as some, but the point of my presenting my personal history is not to offer a comparison to anyone reading this. I share this only to offer how my experience shaped my identity, which led me to self-destruct. However, God offers us a better way of using our sensations and perceptions to organize our experiences toward a more God-centered identity.

Yet God's perception of me is not dependent on me.

I spent a lot of time in high school focusing on myself—my past, my problems, my questions of self-worth. Yet God's perception of me is not dependent on me. He does not see me and choose to love me based on my past, my problems, or my self-worth. He chooses to love me because He is love. Love is inherent in His character, and nothing I do can earn or detract from His love for me. It seems silly now to characterize myself according to things God does not even take into consideration.

Jesus died on the cross for our sins so we do not have to be defined by our pasts.

We all have a past whether distant or recent, but our past does not define our identities. Jesus died on the cross for our sins so we do not have to be defined by our pasts. Without Jesus, we would be undeserving of grace or mercy; but by God's grace, Jesus took on all of our sins and filled our depraved state with His righteousness.

Joseph gives us a fine example of how God transforms lives. Although he was held captive in prison for years for a crime he didn't commit, he experienced a life of fruitfulness and leadership in Egypt. Joseph said he called his firstborn son Manasseh because "God has made me forget all my hardship and all my father's house" (Genesis 41:51). He said he called his second son Ephraim, "For God has made me fruitful in the land of my affliction" (Genesis 41:52).

Here, we see how God not only makes Joseph so fruitful that he forgets his past, but we also see that there is fruit in the future. Now I am not saying that everyone is going to have a prosperous life if he or she follows Jesus. He never promises that this life will be easy. However, we can trust that our future with Jesus in heaven will be greater than anything we can fathom with our earthly minds. The fruit of that kind of future is something we can cling to and hope in as we persevere through difficult situations. Rather than grappling with our past and using the negative aspects of our sinful decisions, we can look to the past of Jesus's sacrifice and see the future that includes an eternal, perfect life with Him.

While we are constructing realities that may not be the most helpful in living a joyful life set on Christ, we can have hope that our future with Jesus will always be better than our past or present. This kind of thinking will change how we organize our sensations and preferences. Rather than using our senses to experience things negatively or perceiving the world through a pessimistic lens, we can use our senses to thank God for gifting us with the ability to have senses that help us perceive the world as just a shadow of our eternal life.

This process is not easy, for older and deeper levels of control are more habitual and difficult to change.[2] This vein of thought rings true with many elements of my own story. Even though I snapped out of my negative thinking toward guys during college, I still found myself repeating old patterns after I graduated because I was suddenly in a different context. This, of course, led to my downfall as I inadvertently placed a lot of my worth in how many guys approached me or expressed interest in me. I did not think of it as a game at the time, but the more attention I received, the more confident I felt in myself.

Confidence in self over confidence in the Creator of self will always lead to destruction.

Confidence is a good thing and a desirable quality to have. However, confidence in self over confidence in the Creator of self will always lead to destruction.

And I was the worst at this.

Because Western society requires presenting our best selves to the world, I learned to do so from an early age. Whether that was making myself marketable in high school for scholarships to pay for college, showcasing my talents to secure jobs, or portraying myself in an appealing way to find a spouse, I had to participate in the confidence game. An employer does not want to hire someone who is not confident in his or her ability to execute job tasks, nor does a husband want a woman who is not confident in herself. A healthy level of confidence is acceptable, but the root of the confidence must ultimately come from Jesus if it is to remain healthy.

174

He designed our past experiences, our present circumstances, and our future conditions. Any excellent thing on a resume is only there because God willed it to be there.

Everything we have is from God, as Romans 11:36 tells us. Therefore, our marketability in an area of life is only marketable because God designed it that way. He designed our past experiences, our present circumstances, and our future conditions. Any excellent thing on a resume is only there because God willed it to be there. Therefore, any confidence in achievement is only through God. Rather than taking in accolades as though we have done it all by our own strengths, we can instead accept compliments with gratitude and glorification of the One who blessed us. How much more could we make God known if we gave Him the glory for every victory He is accomplishing in our lives?

We may be prone to stealing His glory out of our need for the world's or our peers' approval, but this kind of seeking will only lead to disappointment, because no one besides God will ever approve of us perfectly.

Thus, confidence can only come through Jesus, and Jesus is the only One who can perfectly make us feel confident in Him. Our worth is secure in the One who tells us He sees us as the "righteousness of God" because of Jesus's death (2 Corinthians 5:21). God does not see our flaws and reject us because of them, nor does He see our successes and approve of us because of them. He looks at us and sees Jesus taking on all of our flaws on the cross and defeating them along with death through His resurrection. He sees Jesus's success and declares Christians as worthy because of Him and Him alone.

When we place our identities in our own confidence and our own abilities, we will not only disappoint others, but we will disappoint ourselves—and often. But what if we could use these disappointments to draw closer to the One who will never disappoint us? What if each time we felt upset with ourselves, we opened the Bible to see how much greater God is? Perhaps then we could begin replacing old habits of shame and guilt with new habits of praise.

Habitual thinking that traces back over the years (and even decades, for many) will not stop overnight. Years of placing hope in accomplishments and success will not disappear with one reading of this book or a few glances at the Bible. We must find our identities in Christ. Any residual feelings of failure that may trace back to childhood will not go away with my telling you to place your worth elsewhere. These long-lasting, deep-rooted habits will be difficult to break.

But we can make it easier on ourselves to think of these habits in a more optimistic fashion. Avoiding negative thinking will create a void in our usual habits, and not much time will pass before the same habits creep in again in an effort to fill that emptiness. However, *replacing* negative thinking with positive thinking will both eliminate the old pattern and replace it with a new one. Therefore, each time we fail (and we will fail—often!), instead of turning to old patterns of emotional turmoil or identity crises, we can turn to the Bible and let new patterns of praise emerge.

> *Therefore, each time we fail (and we will fail-often!), instead of turning to old patterns of emotional turmoil or identity crises, we can turn to the Bible and let new patterns of praise emerge.*

We can start with the Psalms, the longest book of the Bible, that declare who God is.

Out of the depths I cry to you, O Lord! O Lord, hear my voice! Let your ears be attentive to the voice of my pleas for mercy! If you, O Lord, should mark iniquities, O Lord, who could stand? But with you there is forgiveness, that you may be feared. I wait for the Lord, my soul waits, and in his word I hope; my soul waits for the Lord more than watchmen in the morning, more than watchmen for the morning. O Israel, hope in the Lord! For with the Lord there is steadfast love, and with him is plentiful redemption. And he will redeem Israel from all his iniquities.

Psalm 130; emphasis added

Of all the chapters in the Bible, we find the longest one

in the Psalms. DeYoung declared about Psalm 119, "Surely it is significant that this intricate, finely crafted, single-minded love poem—the longest in the Bible—is not about marriage or children or food or drink or mountains or sunsets or rivers or oceans, but about the Bible itself."[3] God knows the richness of His Word, and that is made clear in Psalm 119.

Developing new patterns of turning to the Bible instead of poor habits may be difficult to accomplish at first, but practicing them regularly can make them into new habits. My hope is not that you place your hope in your ability to fulfill those new patterns; my hope is for Christians to turn to God's Word and find security in Him and Him alone, even if that means turning to Him in the failure of turning to Him perfectly.

Furthermore, one of the most beautiful aspects of being a Christian is the ability to have a new life. Without Jesus, these new patterns of reflecting on God's goodness would not be possible or natural. However, Jesus gives us a new life through His death and resurrection.

We know that our old self was crucified with him in order that the body of sin might be brought to nothing, so that we would no longer be enslaved to sin. For one who has died has been set free from sin.

Romans 6:6–7

We have died to sin and now live *aware* of the sinful nature in which we lived before. We now have the ability to seek Jesus and find life in Him and Him alone. Enslavement to the old patterns of sin and pervasive pessimistic thinking is destroyed; we have freedom in Jesus. We can rejoice that we even have the grace to seek righteousness and new patterns of turning to Him for our hope and comfort. The Christian life is not about performing perfectly or even seeking God perfectly; it is and always will be all about Jesus's perfect sacrifice for us so that we no longer have to be perfect.

"And I am sure of this, that he who began a good work in you will bring it to completion at the day of Jesus Christ" (Philippians 1:6). God is working in us to bring about holiness within the Church. Even though we are far from perfect, we know that God is daily bringing us closer to a perfect future in heaven where we will be free of the sins that try to tempt us away from Him. Until then, we can practice turning to Him instead of turning to ourselves, and ultimately, we can know that His Son will always trump our failures and repetition of old, sinful patterns. Praise God for His grace and mercy that will never cease.

Lending a Preferential Lens

After the accident and my battle with self-image, I knew my lifestyle did not honor God. However, I was unsure of how to engage in a more positive way of living.

Then I started graduate school, and as I have previously mentioned, the university I attended taught this approach to therapy called solution-focused brief therapy (SFBT). One unique aspect of SFBT is that it does not focus on the past. Many people have these preconceptions of therapy as someone lying on the couch retelling their entire family of origin story to a therapist. SFBT does not particularly recommend this technique, although a solution-focused therapist should always do what is most helpful to the client, regardless of the therapist's preferred approach. Instead, SFBT focuses on the presence of current positive behaviors and on clients' preferred futures. I find a lot of this manner of thinking particularly helpful when processing identity as it relates to faith.

I recognize that I have spent a great deal of time talking about my past experiences, but what I do not want to do is dwell on them. SFBT does not focus on the past, unless the client thinks it is helpful, of course—because the client is always the expert on his or her life. The past is not necessarily irrelevant, but an SFBT therapist does not usually see spending time on the past to be as helpful as spending time on the present and the future (at least, that is true in many cases). Therefore, dwelling on my past behaviors and sinful patterns is not helpful to me. It is all relevant to the person I am today and the woman I am continually becoming, but focusing on the guilt of my past will only detract me from leaning on my preferred future of holiness with Jesus. I only bring up my past experiences to showcase how much hope I have in what God is doing to redeem my past for His glory and my good.

We perceive our realities based on what we want to see, so let's make what we see what God wants to see.

What's Wrong with Being Confident?

Our preferences also influence our realities. If we prefer to see the world through a helpful lens, we will begin to see a preferred future.[4] This means that the way we perceive our reality is a direct result of our preferences. We see what we look for; we prefer to see certain things, and therefore, they are a certain way. Of course, this concept only goes so far, as each person's preferences make up a reality that connects everyone's preferences. But we can use the age-old saying (and Hannah Montana's profound lyrics) to discover that "life's what you make it." And the next line of her song resonates with SFBT: "So let's make it rock." We perceive our realities based on what we want to see, so let's make what we see what God wants to see.

However, rather than creating a reality of preferences that lean on self or the flesh, we can create a reality of preferences that honor God.

> *Finally, brothers, whatever is true, whatever is honorable, whatever is just, whatever is pure, whatever is lovely, whatever is commendable, if there is any excellence, <u>if there is anything worthy of praise, think about these things</u>.*
>
> Philippians 4:8; emphasis added

The One worthy of all praise is Jesus. As we begin to see the world through a preferred lens of seeing Jesus's sovereign hand at work in our reality, we will find more and more reasons to praise Him. And as we praise Him, He becomes our joy.

He is at work in and among us,
but we may never see His hand
if we never look for Him.

The way to a more positive and joy-filled way of thinking and living springs from seeing Jesus in the mundane. God is not deistic—uninvolved in His Creation. He is at work in and among us, but we may never see His hand if we never look for Him. However, once we examine our reality with a preference in mind of finding God, we will find Him doing good work among His people.

I could also say the same about the flip side of these statements. If you look for evil, you will find evil because Satan is working, too. But looking for evil and sin isn't helpful, for Satan will have no victory over God. Both 1 Corinthians 6:12 and 1 Corinthians 10:23 discuss the difference between things that are lawful and things that are helpful. Even if "all things are lawful," as these Scripture passages say, the moral relativist might argue that not all things are helpful. God instructs us through both Hebrews 10:24 and 1 Thessalonians 5:11 to encourage one another and stir one another on toward good works. Why, then, would we look for reasons to discourage?

My reality began to shift from one of discouragement to one of encouragement when I started seeing how God was using my sins and frustrations to teach me about my own identity in Him. As I saw His hand working in my life— even through the difficult times—I learned to trust in His plan more than my own. I began to prefer a life centered on Christ rather than a life focused on me. And as a result, I began to find more joy in my life.

Even the hiccups of PTSD could not prevail against God's faithful provision of joy. The trauma was oppressive, but those feelings of fear and unexplainable sadness did not last long. As I began to trust in God more than my feelings, I found Him carrying me through the sadness and bringing me to the other side—victory. This victory after a difficult battle solidified my dedication to seeing God in my reality on a more habitual basis.

I am far from perfect, but I am now relying on Him daily for reminders of His grace and eternal goodness. I know I will fail; perfection is unattainable this side of heaven. But I know He is working in me to produce a good work for His glory. I find myself daily clinging more tightly to His grace over my strength. And I have found this reality to be one I hope I always choose over sin, for my awareness of God's love continually stirs my affections more deeply, daily fulfilling the preferred future that God has for me.

Reflect:
- ☐ What are your favorite habits that you do?
- ☐ What habits annoy you?

Practice:
- ☐ So I obviously had some negative habits and patterns that I entertained for years. However, God interrupted my pattern and taught me some positive

habits to replace the negative ones. I wonder, which of your beliefs are actually lies and what promises of God's truth can replace them.

Chapter Twelve
Where Rivers Flow

Months after the accident, I sat through another one of my graduate school evening classes, listening to the speaker—Dr. April Brown, Director of Veterans Services at Texas Christian University—and avidly taking notes on her ideas of identity. I had never heard the idea that someone can have multiple identities, so I listened with utmost attention.

She discussed how identity changes across time. With each day that passes, we grow into ourselves more and more, learning more about how we function and what our strengths are. Therefore, as we grow, our identities fluctuate.

In addition, she talked about identity as having multiple facets rather than just one. We all have different gifts and different experiences, which lend to different aspects of our identities. Yes, Christians have one identity in Christ as part of the Church, but each person has a different identity under that umbrella. God created us uniquely; even identical twins who have the same DNA are two different people with different preferences. Each person has a different identity that has multiple facets, but as Christians, all facets of that identity flow from our ultimate identity in Christ.

For example, when people ask me about myself, I may say that I am a counselor, an older sibling, a writer, and a Type A person, to name only a handful of identities. However, I know that I can only say each of these identities because of God's grace to me. He gifted me with every aspect of my identity.

However, all these many facets of my life may shift or have different meanings as I grow and develop as a Christian. But my identity in Jesus will always be solid. The faithfulness that He has shown me throughout my endeavors will never change. I know that my faith comes from a place of trusting in God's faithfulness, and that is something solid on which to base my joy—something my own achievements can neither create nor fulfill.

The people in my life may come and go, whether by choice or by the way the world works, but God will never leave. I can always count on Jesus to be immanent in my life as He works His sovereign will for His glory and my good.

I do not have to compare myself to others because Jesus declares me worthy of saving.

Similarly, my health will have its ups and downs. I cannot and will not base my self-worth on my body. First, it is mortal and will pass away when God calls me to heaven. Second, with age, my body's metabolism will decrease (I know this because it is already happening— Lord, help me!). And third, someone will always have better health than I do. Even the fittest fitness junkies compare themselves to others and feel inferior. The prettiest women go to great lengths to enhance their beauty. But Jesus looks at me and declares me beautiful because I have been redeemed by Him and Him alone. I do not have to compare myself to others because Jesus declares me worthy of saving. And since His saving my soul is the cornerstone of my identity, nothing else contributes to my worth more than His salvation.

Thus, approval from others will have no hold over my joy. Sometimes people will approve and commend me for what they deem successful, but most of the time, I fall short of the world's standards. Someone will always be smarter, wiser, and better than I am. But God approves of me because Jesus took on all my sin and conquered it. I can view all my shortcomings as opportunities to glorify God even more.

But [Jesus] said to me, "My grace is sufficient for you, for my power is made perfect in weakness." Therefore, I will boast all the more gladly of my weaknesses, so that the power of Christ may rest upon me. For the sake of Christ, then, I am content with weakness, insults, hardships, persecutions, and calamities. For when I am weak, then I am strong.

2 Corinthians 12:9–10

As we work to maintain this treasure of an identity and as we work to fervently protect it, we have a goal in mind that drives our perseverance. That goal is to find our joy and satisfaction in God alone as we make His name known among our communities. As we rely more on His view of us than our own views of ourselves, we learn more about His holy character and strive to please Him. As we develop a fuller view of who Jesus is and what He has done for us, we grow more thankful for the new life He gives and more gracious to others and ourselves. As we turn our attention more to God and less on ourselves, we will find a joy that will not disappoint but will be steadfast regardless of our circumstances.

To reach this goal, each Christian will have a different approach. Some may avoid whatever distracts them from God (e.g., ungodly music, television, apps, etc.). Some may open the Bible and start a regular plan to seek fulfillment in His Word. And some may get connected to a church group and find the resources and strength to share Jesus with people who do not believe. Because God created us each uniquely, we will have different ways of turning to Jesus.

Therefore, we should praise God when we do anything that takes us one step closer to finding and maintaining a solid identity in Jesus. Regardless of whether the step is small or large, that step is equally important in bringing a Christian closer to dependence on God.

As Christians, we can rest in the idea that success—the way to get where we want to be—is only one option of many ways to reach a goal instead of the only way to get to that goal.[1] Of course, this idea may be true regarding the many ways of reaching goals, but there is only one way of reaching God. "Jesus said to [Thomas], 'I am the way, and the truth, and the life. No one comes to the Father except through me'"

(John 14:6). Therefore, knowing Jesus is the only way we can have access to God. And that is because of Jesus's sacrifice for us, His taking on our sins so that we can come to the Father. Because of God's perfect holiness, we would not have the ability to speak to God if it were not for the forgiveness of our sins. We would be too unholy to access a holy God. However, Jesus (and no one else) grants us this access, and that is why we place our hope in Him and Him alone.

The truth of Jesus is the only way we can draw near to God, but there are many ways to draw near to God through Jesus. That is why we may have many successes or many ways of succeeding as we move to a fuller relationship with Jesus. God gives us endless ways of connecting with Him because He is omnipotent in the universe and immanent in our identities.

In different seasons of life, I have found different success stories that all sprouted from Jesus's work in my heart. As a high schooler, I spent a lot of time outside because my family and I lived in the country. I saw God's magnificent hand in the abundance of stars and the intricacies of pebbles along a river. I cried out to God in the midnight hours as I sought obedience amid constant struggles with my relationships, both at home and at school. These moments were raw and necessary for someone who struggled with locking away her emotions as though they did not exist. God used my midnight prayers to soften my heart and mold my spirit to depend on Him rather than myself.

In another season, I blogged frequently. Every day, I wrote about something God had taught me. I was determined to see God in the mundane, and writing about it verified what I was seeing while giving me an opportunity to use my passions for God's glory. Blogging gave me a chance to journal my thoughts for others to see. Rather than suppressing anything God was teaching me, I published His teachings in my personal life, which also solidified His power in my faith story.

God has also lured me closer to Him through His Word. I have spent many seasons of my life seeking to better understand certain aspects of theology, hermeneutics, and the context of certain books of the Bible. These seasons have involved a more intellectual aspect of my relationship with God, but having a deeper understanding of Scripture has resulted in a deeper understanding of God's character. As I have learned more and more about God, I have also learned how much I need Jesus daily, which helps as I strive to increase Jesus in my life and decrease myself (John 3:30).

Seeing other Christians seeking Him in their lives has inspired me to do the same.

I have also been in seasons where I have drawn closer to Jesus through my community. Since I have had seasons without biblical community, I have relished the times when people have pointed me more to Jesus than to myself. Seeing other Christians seeking Him in their lives has inspired me to do the same. Surrounding myself with people with whom I can both have fun and have serious conversations has blessed my relationship with God immensely.

These are only a handful of ways that Jesus has wooed my heart, and I know He has drawn me closer in many more ways. Christianity is not legalistic, so there are many ways to seek joy in Jesus. And in finding joy in Jesus, we also find a secure identity, which will result in a full life of not worrying about the temptations that draw us away from the cross. Instead, we will live lives that are less run by sin and more directed by the love and grace of Jesus. And that kind of life is, indeed, much sweeter and much more satisfying than any life without Jesus.

Out of Control

I have always been a safe driver. Perhaps it is my Type A coming out, or maybe it is because my mother was always overprotective of me. Regardless, I always double check my mirrors, use my blinkers, and stop completely at stop signs (yes, even when no one is watching). I like the rules of the road, and I want to follow them because I have a fear and respect of driving.

This desire to obey road rules is much like my desire to obey God. Fearing God is healthy, for He is a mighty God—the Creator of the universe who holds our souls in His hands. He is sovereignly in control of designing our lives in ways we cannot fathom. Respecting God is equally healthy, for our sinful desires long to tempt us away. The more we respect Him and how great He is, the more we will also respect the rules that we find in His Word. Both fear and respect come from a place of deep appreciation. The more I appreciate what God has done for me through sacrificing His Son regardless of my sinful nature, the more I appreciate the rules He has put in place for my good. I can trust God and know that anything that occurs in life is what He purposes for His glory and my good. Jesus died for my good. He took on my sin for my good. He daily advocates for me for my good. Any and all rules that God instills are for my good.

The rules of the road are also for my good. I fear the fact that vehicles speed past me; I respect that vehicles can harm me if used improperly. But I also appreciate that vehicles can get me from place to place with much higher speeds than if I did not drive. Therefore, I want to follow the rules because I want to both stay alive and keep driving.

But not everyone who has this same desire to obey the rules of the road has a desire to obey God. Both analogies align with the fact that unilateral control is, at best, an illusion.[2] This reality could either freeze us in fear or inspire us to obey with joy.

Living a life with an identity secured by Jesus is not a common way of living. Non-Christians and even some Christians place an identity in self higher than an identity in Jesus. But this reality does not limit what we can control. Although we cannot control other drivers or other people in general, we can control how we choose to live. We do not have to live in fear of being irrelevant or uncool to non-Christians, "for God gave us a spirit not of fear but of power and love and self-control" (2 Timothy 1:7). We can, instead, choose to be even more like Jesus and care for non-Christians all the more. Jesus said, "I came not to call the righteous, but sinners" (Mark 2:17; see also Matthew 9:12 and Luke 5:31). We can be "the salt of the earth" and "the light of the world" (Matthew 5:13–14). We do not have to shrink back into the darkness after which so many people lust, but we can showcase Jesus's light by accepting that our lives are hidden by Jesus (Colossians 3:3).

We obey Him because that is how we show our love for Him (1 John 5:3). But just as my obedience to the rules of the road falters whenever I am running late to an important meeting, my obedience to God often falters. Paul, the author of much of the New Testament, encourages me by his confession: "For I do not understand my own actions. For I do not do what I want, but I do the very thing I hate" (Romans 7:15). Even someone as spiritually strong as Paul faltered in his sin. No Christian will reach perfection here on earth, but Jesus is sanctifying us for the day we reach heaven. That is why it is imperative for us, as believers, not to first seek obedience to God, but to first rest in Jesus. Even in our obedience, we will fail. But Jesus will never fail. We can cling to Him and hope in Him when we inevitably fail as we live in full surrender to Him.

So live for Jesus! Hide your identity in Jesus so that everyone sees His perfect and unending love when they look at you. But also take comfort in failure because we all are going to fall short. It is in our failures that God's power is made perfect (2 Corinthians 12:9) because we know He will never fail.

I have sought after acceptance, perfection, approval, glory, respect, and riches, yet they have all pointed me more to my failures than my strengths. These ideals were idols that I had placed on the highest pedestal. I tried to construct myself as complete by striving to reach the top of my class, grade, university, and work community, but there was always someone better. And even when I did succeed, I looked to the next part of myself to fix, the success proving empty when the glory faded and when I realized how fleeting worldly gratification is.

I have discovered that any sense of self we create is faulty unless God receives all the glory, for anything that does not give glory to God is short-lived and in need of constant refilling. But God says, "I will make rivers flow on barren heights, and springs within the valleys. I will turn the desert into pools of water, and the parched ground into springs" (Isaiah 41:18 NIV).

God will complete that emptiness in your spirit or the aching for wholeness in your soul.

God will be faithful to overcome any insecurity with which you struggle. God will complete that emptiness in your spirit or the aching for wholeness in your soul. The foundation on which you have built your identity and sense of self may be cracking from lack of the living water, but Jesus is beckoning, "Whoever drinks of the water that I will give him will never be thirsty again. The water that I will give him will become in him a spring of water welling up to eternal life" (John 4:14). God grants eternal healing and fulfillment, and He is faithful to provide, even when every other lie of insecurity or worldly foundation is shaking. As we rely on and trust in God's view of who we are, we continually allow Him to reconstruct our identities around Jesus—the only One who can provide the constant, foundational, and lasting truth needed to flourish in a postmodern world.

Appendix
Accepting the Bible as True

Despite my refusal to think, act, and behave like a typical girl, I finally succumbed to the dismal realization that I, in fact, was thinking, acting, and behaving like a typical girl. I finally broke down and cried about my newfound inability to exercise, a side effect of the wreck's impact that persisted in bruising not only my lungs but also my ego. I had never wanted my appearance to be the center of my happiness, but there I was, letting my insecurities get the best of me, like a typical girl.

I hated every minute of my recovery, but I felt helpless to stop the tears and complaints that flowed forth to my poor roommate. Ashamed, I confessed to her my frustration with the weight that seemed to keep piling onto my love handles. Then she replied with the common words we have all said and heard at some point: "You're not fat."

At that moment, we came to a minor disagreement, for we obviously had two different truths. My truth was my family's car accident had prevented me from exercising, leading my muscles to deteriorate and fat to accumulate. I could see the number on the scale increasing and the reflection in my mirror expanding; I had empirical evidence. She, on the other hand, saw me healing from my wounds and trying to be as healthy as I could be, given the circumstances, pointing out that I was far from being heavier than the average weight for a person of my gender, age, and stature; she had logical evidence.

So which of us was correct in our truth claims? My context consisted of my own understandings of what I believed to be healthy, and her context involved her concept of what she believed to be healthy. Neither contexts were untrue, yet we held fast to different conclusions.

For anyone looking to maintain an identity that prevails beyond fluctuations on the scale, we must find the kind of truth that is more stable than the number on a scale. We need something more secure, something absolute. But looking for absolutes may seem tricky, for what surpasses personal experience? What can argue against one's feelings?

A postmodern thinker may say that one cannot argue against another person's feelings. No one can tell anyone that his or her experience was incorrect, just like my roommate could not nullify my experience of feeling insecure about my appearance. However, where does that leave us? What conclusion do we draw if we want a solid foundation on which to base our understandings, regardless of perspective? Feelings and experiences are subjective; but if we want to stop settling for unstable identities, we have to find an objective answer on which to construct our realities. Otherwise, our identities will remain subject to subjective experiences, which will never provide the stability needed to keep from falling into an identity crisis that comes with shifting opinions.

All these questions and musings follow the postmodern thoughts that led me to discovering what truth is true across all contexts and feelings.

Objectivity and Truth

Postmodernists often claim that "a 'truth' in one context may not be 'truth' in another."[1] As we build an identity that is stable in the Lord, though, we must develop a truth that holds true regardless of one's context.

In matters of truth, the terms *objectivity* and *subjectivity* unavoidably arise. As we seek truth, we also seek objectivity. However, I understand that postmodern thought may claim that objectivity does not exist because each person experiences objectivity differently, making it subjective. To this, I must respond in two ways.

First, I agree with Copan when he says, "To deny the possibility of *any* truth statements or *any* objectivity is to declare the following a true and objective fact: It is *objectively true* that we cannot know something as objectively true."[2] Thus, truth is, in fact, inescapable even when one is denying truth. Therefore, rather than holding to the postmodern idea that truth is nonexistent, we can embrace the availability of truth to some extent.

However, if Copan's response is not sufficient, then I will concede that my experiences with the absolute truth of the Bible are subjective. But across nations, eras, and social strata, the same truth holds true in content.

Everyone's subjective experience of truth does not lessen or weaken the content of the truth, as Copan also observes:

> How does my sincerely believing something make it true? Had it been false before and then it became true? . . . Why not, instead, accept the commonsense intuition we share and live by each day—that things are true or false whether we believe them or not? After all, sincerely believing won't make rush hour traffic or mounting utility bills go away! If we're honest, we have to admit that many things are not under our control.[3]

Similarly, my roommate's and my differing opinions did not annul the facts of the matter. We may have disagreed, but if we had turned to the Bible, we would have found something objective across centuries rather than something as subjective as opinion. Of course, the disagreement was no argument; she was only consoling my girlish insecurities, as any good roommate should do (and preferably, with pizza and ice cream). I am sure she probably pointed me to Scripture, but I likely acted in stubbornness and clung to the lies of my downcast perceptions rather than opening my ears to truth.

Moving forward, I will discuss Who serves as our foundational identity. Then we can look at what truth is and why it crosses all contexts.

Evidence for God

Although I grew up learning about Jesus, I did not fully trust Him with my life until I went to college. I had gone to youth group and thought I knew Jesus throughout middle school and high school, but I did not commit all my ways to God until I finally saw the gospel for what it really was.

The gospel is this: Jesus Christ, who is God in the flesh, descended from heaven and lived a sinless life so He could sacrifice Himself perfectly through taking on the sins of His people by means of His death and through His victory over our sin in His resurrection.

Christians believe the gospel is true through faith and only by the grace of God, but many non-Christians do not believe the gospel because they neither believe in God's existence nor do they believe that the Bible is God's Word. Those who have not tasted the goodness of God believe "the word of the cross is folly" (1 Corinthians 1:18). Therefore, my hope is that the evidence I present will showcase the reality that Jesus is Lord, Creator of the universe, and author of the Bible.

First, God exists, and not even science contradicts that truth, despite popular belief. Francis Collins, physician, geneticist, and leader of the Human Genome Project (which maps out human DNA), believes in God and is a devout Christian, although he grew up not knowing or caring to know about God. Although I am unsure of how the universe began, I know others have researched the matter extensively. Collins, after intrinsic study of the origins of the universe, came to the following conclusion about what science says about the Big Bang Theory:

> The Big Bang cries out for a divine explanation. It forces the conclusion that nature had a defined

beginning. I cannot see how nature could have created itself. Only a supernatural force that is outside of space and time could have done that.[4]

Willaim Lane Craig also addresses the concept that the plausibility of the Big Bang does not detract from the fact that a Creator had to create the circumstances in order for the Big Bang to occur:

What caused the big bang? The Christian maintains that the universe could not have come into existence uncaused out of nothing. This is metaphysically impossible. Out of nothing, nothing comes. Being cannot come from nonbeing. But if a powerful, personal Creator exists, this conundrum evaporates: "In the beginning God created the heavens and the earth" (Gen. 1:1).[5]

Furthermore, it is difficult to believe that our universe could have come to fruition as it did without an intelligent mind being involved. Vincent Carroll and David Shiflett used John Polkinghorne's term *interplay of chance* when they stated, "A number of physicists believe the 'interplay of chance' necessary to create a universe capable of nurturing conscious life is so wildly improbable as to raise questions about why it happened."[6] The scientific community cannot explain why or how the universe came to support life in the manner that it does:

Perhaps life and the universe are inclined toward

anthropocentric features for reasons of structure we do not yet know. But I see a strong possibility intelligent design is present. To get around the anthropocentric universe without invoking God may force you to extreme speculation about there being billions of universes. Positing that essential features of the natural world are explained by billions of variables that cannot be observed strikes me as much more free-wheeling than any of the church's claims.[7]

As much as science aligns with Christianity, Collins makes a valid point that science will not answer all questions about God:

It also became clear to me that science, despite its unquestioned powers in unraveling the mysteries of the natural world, would get me no further in resolving the question of God. If God exists, then He must be outside the natural world, and therefore the tools of science are not the right ones to learn about Him. Instead, as I was beginning to understand from looking into my own heart, the evidence of God's existence would have to come from other directions, and the ultimate decision would be based on faith, not proof.[8]

Similarly, C. S. Lewis discusses the matters of the heart, which Collins also describes as being central to the faith process rather than matters of logic. Lewis explains how things of this life will always leave us wanting more. We will always be hungry again and in need of refilling. We may experience the best day of our lives, but the next day will come, and we will again want more.

But why is this? Why do we long for something more? Lewis claims, "If I find in myself a desire which no experience in this world can satisfy, the most probable explanation is that I was made for another world."[9] Copan also addresses this deep need of the human heart:

> Perhaps our deep unfulfilled desires can help show us that we were made for something no earthly thing can satisfy. . . . If we live in a fallen world, alienated from God, this is no wonder. God has "set eternity in the hearts" of us all (Eccles. 3:11) so that we will be satisfied with nothing less than God alone.[10]

Contrary to the ideas of Collins, Lewis, and Copan, many non-Christians (and Christians, for that matter) cling to the belief that science holds the answers to all questions and that science, in itself, is the most reliable and concrete subject available. People see Christianity and religion as some sort of gray area in which they do not want to meddle. However, has not science changed and progressed over the centuries, whereas the Bible has not? Science declared that the earth was flat, but praise God, scientists have long ago discovered evidence to clear the air on that matter. However, nothing has come to light that has disproved the Bible; in fact, discoveries such as the Dead Sea Scrolls have only confirmed the validity of biblical text. Long before the

Dead Sea Scrolls were discovered, Jewish scholars called the Masoretes had preserved biblical texts for about 400 years, from AD 600 to AD 1000. The Masoretes maintained the practice of counting the words of the texts to make sure each copy of the biblical text was accurate. Furthermore, the Dead Sea Scrolls contained biblical texts from 200 BC to AD 68, which predated the Masoretic texts. Therefore, "because of [the Scrolls'] age and close similarity with the Masoretic Text, we now have an objective basis for determining that the biblical text used in our modern copies of the Old Testament is accurate."[11] The Bible has remained constant, despite the fluctuations of scientific knowledge.

Furthermore, this point may also answer questions as to why scientific details of past events and mathematical certainties are not part of the biblical narrative.

> Long before modern science was born, St. Augustine gave excellent advice to Christians when he said in effect, "We should not rush headlong to one opinion or the other, because there is always the possibility that a hastily adopted viewpoint can turn out to be false, and if our faith is dependent on that view it can appear false, too. And we will be arguing for our own opinions rather than the real doctrines of Scripture."[12]

Thus, although scientists may make discoveries that add to our present knowledge of the universe, God does not include scientific certainties in the biblical canon, likely because science is constantly changing. As humanity seeks knowledge and further understanding of how the natural world operates, new technology and research become available. Those who penned the words of the Bible did not have the resources we have today or the resources people will have hundreds of years from now. Therefore, the writers could not give empirical evidence because they did not yet know the evidence to portray. Thus, the Bible does not include scientific theories because changeable text conflicts with the unchanging Word of God.

A Trustworthy Account

So we are trying to find an objective answer to our questions about identity. Christians believe that those answers are in the Bible alone. Those who hold to moral relativity may disagree with Christian claims of the Bible being God's Word, but their disagreement only shows that they hold their view in higher esteem than Christians' beliefs.[13] So which is correct? "But we recognize that some interpretations are better or more plausible than others. And if this is so, then we assume that one interpretation—or at least a range of interpretations—better conforms to the truth than others.[14]

Simon Greenleaf, a lawyer and jurist, claims similar findings:

> In all human transactions, the highest degree of assurance to which we can arrive, short of the evidence of our own senses, is that of probability. The most that can be asserted is, that the narrative is more likely to be true than false; and it may be in the highest degree more likely, but still be short

of absolute mathematical certainty. . . . For it is by such evidence [that which is sufficient to satisfy a reasonable man] alone that our rights are determined, in the civil tribunals; and on no other evidence do they proceed, even in capital cases.[15]

Therefore, if one truth presides over the other in court—the place where we uphold justice to the highest degree—then why would not a more plausible or probable truth preside in matters of faith?

Paul Little, quoting E. J. Carnell, also introduces the possibility that some ideas may be more probable and more likely to be true in both science and Christianity:

There is a close parallel between science and Christianity which surprisingly few seem to notice. As Christianity *assumes* that all in the Bible is supernatural, so the scientist *assumes* that all in nature is rational and orderly. Both are hypotheses based, not on all of the evidence, but on the evidence "for the most part." Science devoutly holds to the hypothesis that all of nature is mechanical, though, as a matter of fact, the mysterious electron keeps jumping around as expressed by what is called *the Heisenberg principle of uncertainty*. How does science justify its hypothesis that all of nature is mechanical, when it admits on other grounds that many areas of nature do not seem to conform to this pattern?[16] The answer is that since regularity is observed in nature "for the most part," the smoothest hypothesis is to assume that it is the same throughout the whole.[17]

John MacArthur goes into detail about how Scripture became Scripture—or how the books of the Bible became part of the canon,[18] as does Greenleaf when he conducts a thorough examination of the Gospels of Matthew, Mark, Luke, and John, which serve as the basis of Christianity.[19] MacArthur verifies the importance of Scripture to faith:

> We cannot have geology without rocks, or anthropology without men. We cannot have a melody without musical notes, nor can we have a divine record of God without His words. Thoughts are carried by words and God revealed His thoughts in words. The very words of Scripture are inspired. Scripture is verbal revelation.[20]

Therefore, if we believe in God, then we believe God's Word is true. And to those who want scientific proof that science aligns with Scripture, MacArthur gives a lengthy list of references for further investigation.[21]

Many have either read or heard about the popular book *A Case for Christ* by Lee Strobel, in which the author investigates the evidence for Jesus. Although he begins his journalistic journey as an atheist, he discovers compelling evidence that Jesus is Lord, as many other atheist-turned-Christian authors have similarly experienced.[22]

Postmodern thought is open to each individual's understanding of reality as being true to that person.

Therefore, rather than shutting down the possibility of the Bible being absolutely true, one would consider what I have found to be true in my experience (both research-based and personal), giving my evidence fair consideration. I do recognize the plausibility of others' experiences that have led them to disbelieve the inerrancy of Scripture and the existence of God; therefore, my hope in writing this book is not to accuse anyone of being wrong. I would much rather show what I have found to be true based on extensive research and the Bible as opposed to less stable ideas.

Strobel discusses one element of proof—archaeology—similar to how I previously discussed my conversation with my roommate: "Archaeology, like most sciences, involves drawing conclusions from evidence. You know as well as I do that two different people can draw two different conclusions from the same evidence."[23] Thus, truth may not be truth in different contexts, for two different perspectives may draw distinct understandings of the same thing. However, the differing perspectives do not alter the content of the observed. Although the observer automatically changes the observed simply through the act of observing, I have yet to see this concept hold true with the written word. Although people who write have their own subjective experiences of the content they write, the content becomes more valid when more people across different contexts write the same thing. Strobel assessed his fact-finding as follows:

I didn't become a Christian because of archaeology, and I wouldn't recommend that anyone else base a faith completely on archaeology, either. Archaeological evidence doesn't *prove* that Jesus is God. What it does do, however, is provide corroborative evidence that the writings about Jesus are trustworthy accounts.[24]

Strobel does not advise anyone to base his or her faith on archaeology, even if "scholars have concluded that no archaeological evidence found to date flat-out contradicts the Bible."[25] Even if this statement is mind-boggling and perhaps convincing in itself, this is just a taste of why the writings of the Bible are trustworthy accounts.

Since being a graduate student, I have read a lot of material, and most of what I have read has to do with solution-focused (SF) therapy. I won't bore you with a detailed explanation of SF therapy; however, it is important to know that this method focuses more on clients' solutions rather than their problems. It is much more efficient and client-centered than some other approaches, but I admit I am fairly biased.

I bring up solution-focused therapy because similar to solution-focused thinking (which falls under the postmodern umbrella), Strobel mentions that "you really can't draw a scientifically valid conclusion one way or the other from the *absence* of archaeological evidence."[26] Just like an SF therapist would focus on the presence of promising behaviors rather than the absence of desired outcomes, those seeking to corroborate the validity of the Bible may want to seek what is present rather than what is not. Despite the fact that the original manuscripts of the Bible were copied into 24,000 New Testament manuscripts to ensure accuracy, the copies said "virtually the same thing." This finding led to Strobel's conclusion that "it makes sense that they are accurate copies of the original," especially when compared with other ancient texts (e.g., Plato's writings, Homer's *Iliad*, etc.) for which we have only 30 and 650 manuscript copies, respectively.[27] Furthermore, despite the vast number of biblical manuscripts that all say the same thing, Strobel found "some variations in spelling and stuff like that, but 99.5 percent of the manuscripts match up."[28] No other text has retained such accuracy across extensive copying and across so many copiers. Thus, regardless of how each person viewed the New Testament manuscripts based on their own experiences, they all say the same thing, showing the validity of the text.

When thinking about the inerrancy of the Bible, my mind perked up to the other 0.05 percent. Being the studious and research-based person that I am, I interviewed some men in my church who have studied the Bible much more intensively than I. Ezra Boggs, founder of the Bible and Beer Consortium,[29] presented answers to my question about the other 0.05 percent.

Using the following example, Boggs posited that the differences in copying only resulted from holes in parchment or other physical obstructions—not differences in opinions. Therefore, we can trust that the content in our Bible today is the same content that was in the Bible when it first entered the canon.

two men ran

two men ran

t o men ran

two men ran

tw men ran

two men ran

wo men ran

In addition, Boggs makes a strong point on the inerrancy of Scripture in that what Scripture affirms, it affirms inerrantly.[30] Even though other sources (e.g., science, etc.) confirm the accuracy of the Bible, Kevin DeYoung makes an excellent point regarding the Bible's authority that portrays the insufficiency of these other sources:

> You can't establish the supreme authority of your supreme authority by going to some other lesser authority. Yes, the logic is circular, but no more so than the secularist defending reason by reason or the scientist touting the authority of science based on science. This doesn't mean Christians can't be irrational and unreasonable in their views, but it does mean our first principle is neither rationality nor reason. We go [to] the Bible to learn about the Bible because to judge the Bible by any other standard would be to make the Bible less than what it claims to be.[31]

Thus, in looking to the Bible to determine its objectivity, we can first look at the authors of the New Testament. As I mentioned before, Greenleaf wrote an extensive book on the validity of the authors of the Gospels of Matthew, Mark, Luke, and John. His thorough examination proved the accuracy and veracity of what they recorded. However, some may believe that what the authors wrote was simply legend, because some believe the writers put forth the texts hundreds of years after Jesus died. Strobel interviewed many scholars on the matter and concluded, "This wasn't 100 years or 50 years or even 30 years after Jesus' death; this was 2 to 5 years after Jesus' death. And experts said that's far too fast for legend to have developed and wiped out a core of historical truth."[32] This accuracy differs from the accuracy of other written works about other highly respected people of historical times. The writings and biographies about Alexander the Great, for example, were not written until 400 years after he died. Those who wrote the inspired text of the New Testament began the process of documenting the truth of the gospels too soon after Jesus's death for their experiences to become folklore. Two authors quote Sir Frederic Kenyon on the matter:

> The interval, then, between the dates of original composition and the earliest extant evidence becomes so small as to be in fact negligible, and the last foundation for any doubt that the Scriptures have come down to us substantially as they were written has now been removed. Both the authenticity and the general integrity of the books of the New Testament may be regarded as finally established.[33]

Greenleaf both affirms the accuracy of these documents and questions any doubt of the documents:

> If any ancient document concerning our public rights were lost, copies which had been as universally received and acted upon as the Four Gospels have been, would have been received in evidence in any of our courts of justice, without the slightest hesitation.[34]

Furthermore, those who wrote the New Testament (including disciples and apostles of Christ) did so with the utmost care in order to uphold the truth they put forth because of the Person of whom they were writing. They were not writing about an ordinary man; they were writing about the God of the universe. "One prominent archaeologist carefully examined Luke's references to 32 countries, 54 cities, and 9 islands, and didn't find a single mistake."[35] The authors of the New Testament did not make errors when recording the events of their context. And any seemingly contradictory observations in the Bible (Jesus's healing of a Roman commander's servant (Matthew 8:5–13; Luke 7:1–10)) and Jesus's genealogies (Matthew 1:1–16; Luke 3:23–28) actually line up with each recorder's context.[36] Strobel mentions that these examples showcase even more the truth of what the authors wrote: "The idea is that if the writers were lying, they'd make sure to get their stores straight—and they'd agree in every detail. What seems to be a contradiction is often just the same event viewed from a different perspective."[37] This comment again aligns with how differing perspectives are inevitable across contexts; however, the different perspectives of the authors of the New Testament do not contradict each other but instead show a more rounded story of Jesus Christ.[38]

I have thus far mentioned information backing up the trustworthiness of the New Testament, but the Old Testament is just as reliable. Second Timothy 3:16 states, "All Scripture is breathed out by God and profitable for teaching, for reproof, for correction, and for training in righteousness." Therefore, because we can trust the New Testament statement that all Scripture is from God, we can trust the account of the Old Testament as well. In addition, when looking at the purpose of the Old Testament, we see that it is all just a foretaste of the New Testament. In the Old Testament, we see the cultural, moral, and ceremonial laws that people had to uphold before approaching God. We also see prophesies. MacArthur stated, "Despite astronomical odds, hundreds of biblical prophecies have come true, and they make the most objective argument for the Bible's authority."[39]

Jesus both fulfilled prophecies and the old lawful requirements, and then He turned these laws into laws of the heart. The Old Testament is just a reflection of who we are without Jesus; the New Testament brings light to who we are because of Jesus. Thus, although many authors have written on the accuracy and reliability of the Old Testament as well, I will spend the majority of my time in the New Testament because of my purpose of writing about our identity in Christ. The Old Testament is helpful for pointing us to our need of a Savior, but our Savior has come and teaches us of His goodness through the New Testament.

In all, moving forward, I have learned to uphold the entire Bible—both New and Old Testaments—as a trustworthy account as we seek to understand the only trustworthy source that turns us back to our foundational identity in Jesus.

Objectivity and Perception

As I caught a glimpse of the red truck flying in front of our Jeep, I heard our driver, a good family friend, utter an obscenity before everything literally spun out of control.

I do not remember the sounds or the feeling of the impact; all I remember is the moment everything went still. This stillness only lasted moments, if that, before my 14-year-old sister spoke. She repeated the phrase "I love you" over and over again, quickly bringing my consciousness back. I noticed my stepdad in the passenger's seat and our family friend fumbling around in the front as my sister said: "I see smoke; get out of the car."

My imagination did not have to travel far as I imagined our Jeep exploding on the side of the road—like something out of a movie. Before I could respond to my mother, who was now asking if everyone was okay, I unbuckled my seatbelt and turned the handle of the doorest nearest me, stumbling out of the car and leaving my purse, phone, and family behind.

The thoughts that ran through my mind in those moments were certainly subjective, but now that I have covered the existence of truth in some detail, I must address the fact that many postmodernists may claim that there is no objective assessment or experience of reality and that we are not capable of perceiving or knowing reality as it actually *is*.[40] Therefore, if we are to find objectivity, we must discover if an objective (unbiased) reality even exists.

While I was inside the confines of the Jeep, I only knew what had happened based on my perspective from the backseat. The driver had a little bit more of an understanding of what happened because he saw it as it was about to happen. The same held true for every other passenger in the Jeep in that each person had a different perspective of the situation as it happened. The driver of the red truck also had a different understanding of what was about to happen. None of us could have an objective stance on the accident while the accident was happening.

However, I would not say that an objective reality did not exist in the situation. Instead, I would say that only Someone outside the situation—before, during, and after the accident—could have an objective understanding of it. That Someone can only be an omnipotent[41] God.

This word *omnipotence* is not something Christians say just because it's a long word and sounds good. God portrays His power through language in His Word. In Jeremiah 32, Jeremiah prayed to God, praising Him for His unlimited power and petitioning for understanding by saying, "Ah, Lord God! It is you who have made the heavens and the earth by your great power and by your outstretched arm! Nothing is too hard for you" (Jeremiah 32: 17). God replies in Jeremiah 32:27, "Behold, I am the Lord, the God of all flesh. Is anything too hard for me?" This statement is consistent with what Jesus said in Matthew 19:26 and what the angel Gabriel said in Luke 1:37, where both heavenly beings declared that nothing is impossible with God.

Isaiah writes of the Lord, saying, "For the Lord of hosts has purposed, and who will annul it? His hand is stretched out, and who will turn it back?" (Isaiah 14:27). God also spoke, proclaiming, "Also henceforth I am he; there is none who can deliver from my hand; I work, and who can turn it back?" (Isaiah 43:13).

These are but a few verses that discuss the total power that only God has. Collins also addresses God's omnipotence and sovereignty as he processes the God of the universe: "If God exists, then He is supernatural. If He is supernatural, then He is not limited by natural laws. If He is not limited by natural laws, there is no reason He should be limited by time. If He is not limited by time, then He is in the past, the present, and the future."[42]

This power stretches over knowledge, sovereignty, and love. And God's omnipotent sovereignty shows that He is the only One who can have an objective stance on reality because He is completely aseitic.[43] He does not base His decisions on preferences, as though He could choose A, B, C, or D on a multiple choice exam. He has Plan A, and no other concept of any other plan exists. He existed before time and during time, and He will exist after time:

> *Lord, you have been our dwelling place in all generations. Before the mountains were brought forth, or ever you had formed the*

*earth and the world, from everlasting to everlasting <u>you are
God</u>. You return man to dust and say, "Return, O children of
man!" For a thousand years in your sight are but as yesterday
when it is past, or as a watch in the night.*

Psalm 90:1–4; emphasis added

Therefore, He is not constrained by anything, not by a
limited perspective or by subjective understandings of reality.
He created the reality in which we have lived, are living, and
will live. Thus, how could He be subject to our feeble grasp
of our own realities? Even if each reality is different for each
individual person, His reality contains all our realities more
than we can even understand them—and more than we can
fathom that is outside of our realities.

C. S. Lewis goes into great depth in *Mere Christianity* about
the forces of the universe and how they make sense only
by including God.[44] In *The Problem of Pain*, Lewis goes into
great detail about God's omnipotence in particular, but this
sentence struck me the most as it relates to God's objectivity:

The freedom of God consists in the fact that *no cause
other than Himself produces His acts and no external obstacle
impedes them*—that His own goodness is the root
from which they all grow and His own omnipotence
the air in which they all flower" (emphasis added).[45]

Thus, although everyone on earth may be limited to a subjective stance no matter the circumstance or situation, only One who is omnipotent over every circumstance and situation could have objectivity.

Thus, although everyone on earth may be limited to a subjective stance no matter the circumstance or situation, only One who is omnipotent over every circumstance and situation could have objectivity. Deuteronomy 10:17 declares God's lack of subjectivity: "For the Lord your God is God of gods and Lord of lords, the great, the mighty, and the awesome God, who is not partial and takes no bribe." God's innate nature, therefore, provides us a solid and concrete source to which we can go for unchanging and perfect counsel.

God knew that the red truck was going to hit our Jeep before He created the universe, and He knew during the wreck that He was going to protect my family and me despite the 50-mile-per-hour impact. He knew that after the wreck, my concept of identity would begin to morph so I could put forth these words I am typing now.

God does not have limits and has the only objective reality in existence, and He speaks to us through the language of the Bible, which is a trustworthy account from which we can derive truth.

We have already discussed how subjectivity is part of human nature and how no one except God can have an objective stance on anything. However, I do want to specifically address the thought that perception and behavior determine beliefs.[46]

When I heard my sister's panicked voice saying words that were more than a little alarming, I did not have to look far to see the smoke to which she was referring. Her behavior caused me to perceive something I had not noticed before: the smoke. However, I did not wait around to see if I smelled fire or gasoline or smoke; instead, my perception of the situation based on my sister's behavior forced me to act before I thought. I am sure some sort of adrenaline was running through my veins, in addition to survival instincts, but I automatically allowed my perception and reactive behavior to influence my beliefs about my circumstance.

We found out later that the "smoke" my sister saw was actually airbag powder. Apparently, airbags commonly have a powder in them that tends to explode upon deployment, but I had not known about airbag powder before the wreck. They never taught me about airbag powder in driver's education. My mom never told me about airbag powder. I did not even know airbag powder existed

> **Airbag Powder = Satan Disguising Himself as an Angel of White**

The possibility of smoke nearby caused me to believe I was in a dire situation, which also triggered me to act in survival mode. Later developments shattered my instantaneous belief system, but the point I want to make here is that, yes, our perceptions and behaviors determine our beliefs, just like my sister's statement about smoke determined my understanding of my situation.

Similarly, the society in which we live provides many opportunities for others to distort our perceptions of ourselves. Specifically, when we consider our peers or authority figures or idols, we perceive them as either better or worse than ourselves, rarely comparing on neutral terms. In addition, our own behaviors and the behavior of others determine either true or untrue self-concepts, thereby adding to the beliefs we allow to rule our minds.

Just as God is the only One who can possess objectivity, He is the only One who can perceive us perfectly.

Thus, if we are to live with an undistorted view of who we are, we cannot neglect the importance of being aware of our perceptions as they relate to behavior and belief. However, although we perceive much in this world, we have Someone who perceives us more consistently than anyone else perceive us. Just as God is the only One who can possess objectivity, He is the only One who can perceive us perfectly. Therefore, when embracing stable identities, we can look both to what God says about us, allowing His perceptions to influence our beliefs, and to what God has done for us, allowing His sacrificial behavior on the cross to speak more into our beliefs than anything else.

Notes

Chapter 1

1. Frank Thomas, *Tenets of Constructivism* (classroom handout, Texas Christian University, 2016).
2. Thomas, *Tenets of Constructivism*.
3. Jonathan Edwards's *An Unpublished Essay on the Trinity* is a detailed essay on God's triune nature.
4. Thomas, *Tenets of Constructivism*.
5. Francis S. Collins, *The Language of God: A Scientist Presents Evidence for Belief* (New York: Free Press, 2006), 53.
6. C. S. Lewis, *The Complete C. S. Lewis Signature Classics* (New York: HarperSanFrancisco, 2002), 21.

Chapter 2

1. Thomas, *Tenets of Social Constructionism* (classroom handout, Texas Christian University, 2016).
2. Ryan Keeney, "A Living Killing" (sermon, The Paradox Church, Fort Worth, Texas, November 1, 2015), http://theparadoxchurch.com/sermons-

archive/?enmse=1&enmse_sid=2&enmse_mid=295.

3. Ibid.

4. Thomas, *Tenets of Social Constructionism.*

5. Paul Copan, *"That's Just Your Interpretation": Responding to Skeptics Who Challenge Your Faith* (Grand Rapids: Baker Books, 2001), 39.

6. Jim Essian, "An Awakened Conscience" (sermon, The Paradox Church, Fort Worth, Texas, April 3, 2016), http://subsplash.com/prdxsermons/s/0b60dce/.

7. Ibid.

8. Ibid.

9. Martin Luther, Diet of Worms, April 18, 1521.

10. Essian, "An Awakened Conscience."

Chapter 3

1. Thomas, *Tenets of Constructivism.*

2. John F. MacArthur, *Why Believe the Bible?* (Ventura, CA: Regal, 1980), 32.

3. Copan, *"That's Just Your Interpretation,"* 37–38.

4. Heinz von Foerster, *The Beginning of Heaven and Earth Has No Name: Seven Days with Second-Order Cybernetics* (New York: Fordham University Press, 2014), 103.

5. Thomas, *Tenets of Constructivism.*

6. Ibid.

7. Humberto Matarana and Francisco Varela, quoted in Robert Kull, *Solitude: Seeking Wisdom in Extremes: A Year Alone in the Patagonia Wilderness* (Novato, CA: New World Library, 2008), 157.

8. Copan, *"That's Just Your Interpretation,"* 38, 42.

Chapter 4

1. Von Foerster, "The Need of Perception for the Perception of Needs," Leonardo 22(2): 223–226, http://www.univie.ac.at/constructivism/archive/fulltexts/1714.html.
2. Ibid.
3. Essian, "Easter 2016" (sermon, The Paradox Church, Fort Worth, Texas, March 27, 2016), http://theparadoxchurch.com/sermons-media/?enmse=1&enmse_sid=2&enmse_mid=319.
4. Ibid.
5. Ibid.
6. C. S. Lewis, *The Problem of Pain*, in *The Complete C. S. Lewis Signature Classics* (New York: C. S. Lewis Pte. Ltd., Harper Collins Publishers, Inc., 2002), 381.
7. Ezra Boggs and Ryan Keeney, interview by Amanda Rutledge, June 21, 2016.
8. Thomas, *Tenets of Constructivism*.

Chapter 5

1. Ezra Boggs, interview by Amanda Rutledge, June 21, 2016.
2. Lewis, *The Complete C. S. Lewis Signature Classics*, 10.
3. Thomas, *Tenets of Social Constructionism*.
4. Von Foerster, in Thomas, *Tenets of Social Constructionism*.

Chapter 6

1. Thomas, *Tenets of Social Constructionism.*
2. Keeney, "Gripped by Love" (sermon, The Paradox Church, Fort Worth, Texas, November 15, 2015), http://theparadoxchurch.com/sermons/genesis/?enmse=1&enmse_sid=26&enmse_mid=299.
3. Thomas, *Tenets of Social Constructionism.*
4. Ryan Griffith, "Confessing Our Sins Together," *Desiring God*, June 26, 2014, accessed August 8, 2016, http://www.desiringgod.org/articles/confessing-our-sins-together.
5. Thomas, *Tenets of Social Constructionism.*

Chapter 7

1. Thomas, *Tenets of Social Constructionism.*
2. Jonathan Edwards, "An Unpublished Essay on the Trinity," *Christian Classics Ethereal Library*, accessed May 22, 2017, https://www.ccel.org/ccel/edwards/trinity/files/trinity.html.
3. Kevin DeYoung, *Taking God at His Word: Why the Bible Is Knowable, Necessary, and Enough, and What That Means for You and Me* (Wheaton: Crossway, 2014), 21.

Chapter 8

1. Essian, Sermon on Genesis 34 (The Paradox Church, February 7, 2016).
2. Paraphrased by Copan, "Your Interpretation," 12, from

Notes

William Lane Craig, "Design and the Cosmological Argument," in *Mere Creation*, ed. William Dembski (Downers Grove, Ill.: InterVarsity Press, 1998), 332–59.

3. Von Foerster, in Thomas, *Tenets of Social Constructionism*.
4. Thomas, *Tenets of Social Constructionism*.

Chapter 9

1. Thomas, *Tenets of Social Constructionism*.
2. Lewis, *The Complete C. S. Lewis Signature Classics*, 9–25.
3. J. P. Moreland, *Scaling the Secular City: A Defense of Christianity* (Grand Rapids: Baker Publishing Group, 1987), 241–242.
4. Ibid., 246.
5. Ibid.
6. Lewis, *The Complete C. S. Lewis Signature Classics*, 380.
7. Essian, "We Are God's Building: Part One" (The Paradox Church, Fort Worth, Texas, July 31, 2016), http://subsplash.com/prdxsermons/v/daceb45.
8. Simon Greenleaf, *The Testimony of the Evangelists* (Grand Rapids: Baker Books, 1984), 4.
9. C. S. Lewis, *The Weight of Glory and Other Addresses* (New York: HarperOne, 1949), 30.
10. Greenleaf, *The Testimony of the Evangelists*, 5–6.
11. Ibid., 42.

Chapter 10

1. Lena Groeger, "Making Sense of the World, Several

Senses at a Time," *Scientific American,* February 28, 2012, accessed June 30, 2016, https://www.scientificamerican.com/article/making-sense-world-sveral-senses-at-time/.

2. Thomas, *Tenets of Constructivism.*
3. Lewis, *The Complete C. S. Lewis Signature Classics*, 381.
4. Ezra Boggs, interview by Amanda Rutledge, June 21, 2016.
5. Saul McLeod, "Information Processing," *Simply Psychology*, 2008, accessed June 30, 2016, http://www.simplypsychology.org/information-processing.html.
6. Ibid.
7. Barton Gingerich, "The Millennial Generation's Acceptable Sin," *The Gospel Coalition*, January 7, 2013, accessed June 30, 2016, https://www.thegospelcoalition.org/article/the-millennial-generations-acceptable-sin.
8. Charles P. Barnard and Bruce P. Kuehl, "Ongoing Evaluation In-Session Procedures for Enhancing the Working Alliance and Therapy Effectiveness," *American Journal of Family Therapy*, Vol. 23(2), 1995, 167.
9. When I refer to lust, I refer to longing for anything more than longing for God.
10. Essian, Sermon on Genesis 34 (The Paradox Church, February 7, 2016).
11. Essian, Sermon on Genesis 25 (The Paradox Church, November 8, 2015).
12. Essian.

Chapter 11

1. Thomas, *Tenets of Constructivism*.
2. Ibid.
3. DeYoung, *Taking God at His Word*, 12.
4. Thomas, *Tenets of Constructivism*.

Chapter 12

1. Thomas, *Tenets of Social Constructionism*.
2. Ibid.

Appendix

1. Thomas, *Tenets of Constructivism*.
2. Copan, "*That's Just Your Interpretation*," 42.
3. Ibid., 39.
4. Collins, *The Language of God*, 67.
5. William Lane Craig, "Design and the Cosmological Argument," in *Mere Creation*, ed. William Dembski (Downers Grove, IL.: InterVarsity Press, 1998), 332–359, quoted in Copan, "*That's Just Your Interpretation*," 12.
6. Vincent Carroll and David Shiflett, *Christianity on Trial: Arguments against Anti-Religious Bigotry* (San Francisco: Encounter Books, 2002), 81.
7. Carroll and Shiflett, *Christianity on Trial*, 82, quoting physicist Charles Townes from Gregg Easterbrook, *Beside Still Waters: Searching for Meaning in an Age of Doubt* (New York: William Morrow & Co., 1998), 78–79.

8. Collins, *The Language of God*, 30.

9. C. S. Lewis, *Mere Christianity* (Westwood: Barbour and Company, 1952), 115.

10. Copan, *"That's Just Your Interpretation,"* 18.

11. Jim Franks, "Is the Bible True? Proof 2: Dead Sea Scrolls," Life, Hope & Truth, accessed August 22, 2016, http://lifehopeandtruth.com/bible/is-the-bible-true/proof-2-dead-sea-scrolls/. (For further readings on the inerrancy of the Bible, see Norman Geisler's *Inerrancy*, 1978; *A General Introduction to the Bible*, 1986; and *From God to Us*, 2012.)

12. John F. MacArthur, *Why Believe the Bible?*, 27.

13. Copan, *"That's Just Your Interpretation,"* 31.

14. Ibid., 32.

15. Greenleaf, *The Testimony of the Evangelists*, 45.

16. In other words, chaos theory, and quantum physics.

17. Paul Little, *Know Why You Believe* (Downers Grove, IL: InterVarsity Press, 1968), 85, quoting E. J. Carnell, *An Introduction to Christian Apologetics* (Grand Rapids: Eerdmans, 1950), 208.

18. MacArthur, *Why Believe the Bible?*, 74–79.

19. Greenleaf also gives a reference for God's gifting of the Word to man: Dr. Hopkins's Lowell Lectures, particularly Lect. 2. Bp. *Wilson's Evidences of Christianity, Vol. I., 45–61. Horne's Introduction, Vol. I.*, 1–39.

20. MacArthur, *Why Believe the Bible?*, 48.

21. John F. MacArthur, *Focus on Fact* (Old Tappan, NJ: Fleming H. Revell Company, 1967), Chaps. 7, 8, and 9; Henry Morris, *Many Infallible Proofs* (San Diego, CA:

Creation-Life Publishers, 1974); Batsell B. Baxter, *I Believe Because* (Grand Rapids, MI: Baker Book House, 1971); Bernard Ramm, *Protestant Christian Evidences* (Chicago: Moody Press, 1953); Harold Lindsell, *God's Incomparable Word* (Wheaton, IL: Victor Books, 1977); James C. Hefley, *Adventures with God . . . Scientists Who Are Christians* (Grand Rapids, MI: Zondervan Publishing House, 1967).

22. Others who have experienced similar transitions: Josh McDowell (*More Than a Carpenter*); Paul Johnson (*Intellectuals*); Mitch Stokes (*How to Be an Atheist*); Francis Collins (Project Head of Human Genome Project); Sean McDowell; Daniel B. Wallace; Simon Greenleaf.

23. Strobel, *The Case for Christ* (Grand Rapids: Zondervan, 1998), 68.

24. Ibid., 69.

25. Ibid., 68.

26. Ibid., 68.

27. Ibid., 62–63.

28. Ibid., 62.

29. The Bible and Beer Consortium holds debates in bars or pubs where a speaker from an atheist perspective and a speaker from a Christian perspective discuss matters of disagreement. For further information, see http://www.thebibleandbeerconsortium.com.

30. Ezra Boggs, interview by Amanda Rutledge, June 21, 2016.

31. DeYoung, *Taking God at His Word*, 24.

32. Strobel, *The Case for Christ*, 60.

33. Sir Frederic Kenyon, *The Bible and Archaeology*, quoted in Paul Little, *Why & What Book* (Wheaton: Victor Books, 1980), 81.

34. Greenleaf, *The Testimony of the Evangelists*, 10.

35. Strobel, *The Case for Christ*, 70.

36. Ibid., 58.

37. Ibid., 54.

38. For more information about each of the points I mentioned, see chapters 5 and 6 of Strobel, *The Case for Christ*.

39. MacArthur, *Why Believe the Bible?*, 36.

40. Thomas, *Tenets of Constructivism*.

41. "Having virtually unlimited authority or influence." *Merriam Webster*, s.v. "omnipotent," accessed June 2, 2017, https://www.merriam-webster.com/dictionary/omnipotent.

42. Collins, *The Language of God*, 81.

43. "Existence originating from and having no source other than itself." *Dictionary.com*.

44. If you have doubts about how God fits in with the universe, I strongly suggest reading Book One (if not all books) from *Mere Christianity* by C. S. Lewis. He devoted an entire book on the subject, which is more time than I seek to spend in my own text.

45. Lewis, *The Complete C. S. Lewis Signature Classics*, 383.

46. Thomas, *Tenets of Constructivism*.

About the Author

Amanda grew up in Waco, Texas, but later moved to Dallas to attend Dallas Baptist University. She graduated in 2015 before beginning graduate school at Texas Christian University in Fort Worth. When she moved, she partnered with Paradox Church, where she met her now-husband, Kevin. She aspires to be a counselor for adolescents while continuing to write, whether through books or her blog. During her five-and-a-half years of post-secondary education, she has learned about psychology and theories of counseling that have shaped how she sees clients. She loves serving people by listening to their stories, and she believes strongly in the redemptive nature of the gospel, no matter how difficult the circumstance. She has certainly seen God prove His faithfulness in her life and wants others to know His grace, and she hopes to make this truth known to all she encounters. You can find Amanda at the following places:

amandarutledge.com
Instagram: @amandarrutledge
Twitter: @amandarrutledge
Facebook: @amandaraschelrutledge